MW00785931

Navajo Taboos

Sidewinder Publishing, LLC
2007

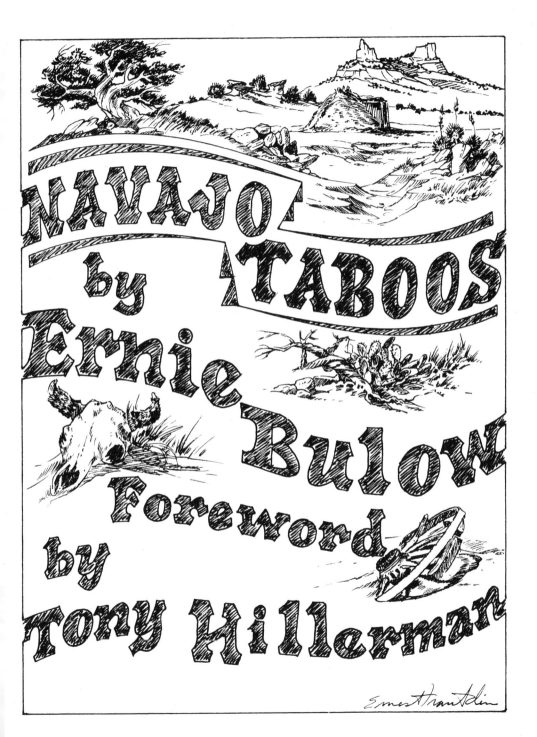

NAVAJO TABOOS

by

Ernie Bulow

Foreword

by

Tony Hillerman

With Special Thanks to My Two Guardian Angels
Tad West and Dale Whale

Navajo Taboos, 2007 by Ernie Bulow and Sidewinder Publishing, LLC

ISBN 978-0-914001-01-0 (paper)
ISBN 978-0-924002-02-7 (cloth)

Sidewinder Publishing
4609 Kinney St. SE
Albuquerque, NM 87105

505-998-8000

www.sidewinderpublishing.com
www.buffalomedicince.com

Dedicated To The

NAVAJO PEOPLE

Especially For My Boys
Curtis Wilson and Frank Silversmith
and all those who died much too young

CONTENTS

A Navajo must stay in harmony with the natural and supernatural worlds

FOREWORD
BY
TONY HILLERMAN

The hardest lesson to learn about people of another race is that they are just like you in all essential ways. They, too, enjoy being warm, dry, well fed, secure, loved by their family and approved of by their friends and neighbors. The cultural differences — whether our taboos relate to belching in public, stepping on the path left by running water, stepping on a crack in the sidewalk, or burning wood from a tree struck by lightning; whether our metaphysical symbols involve masks or incense or hymns or chants — are peripheral matters which do not depend on genetics.

They are products of economics, geography and religion and not our blood — matters of fashion rather than biological inheritance.

Ernie Bulow and I both happened to learn that simple but difficult lesson as children when learning such things is relatively easy because we have not yet been taught that overwhelming false premise that racial characteristics make people fundamentally different. I learned it growing up with Potawatomie and Seminole kids as my neighbors, playmates, teammates, schoolmates, cotton pickers and fellow rabbit hunters. Ernie learned it working in the sugar beet fields with the Navajo families who came to Idaho as hired hands on his family's small farm.

"I had more in common with the Navajos I worked with than I did with my cousins from Chicago — and still do," Ernie says. "I'm not an anthropologist nor ethnologist. I have never "studied" Navajos in any scholarly sense. I have just lived next to them most of my life and cared enough to pay attention to their culture. I stay in Gallup because I love the country and the people, not because it's the best place to live, or to make a living."

The same characteristics of the Navajo Way appeal to both Ernie and me. It is usually wrong to generalize about any group, but I feel safe in saying that the average Navajo has a lively sense of humor, a talent for self-mockery, a wide and warm streak of generosity, and more appreciation for beauty than the average American.

Navajos value people above things, the individual over material goods, far more than does the dominant Anglo-American culture. A traditional Navajo gains no status by accumulating possessions. In fact wealth may be taken as evidence one is neglecting his most important responsibility — caring for his relatives. Nor is status gained in the fierce

12

Ceremonies are used to restore balance

competitiveness that marks the American Way. In the Navajo Way, one who wins too often must find a way to give others a better chance. I know a Navajo rodeo rider who won three consecutive competitions and then took care not to win again for the rest of the season. Moderation in all things might be the motto of the traditional Navajo culture.

Some of the taboos you will encounter here involve this emphasis on moderation. Others reflect the high value the Navajo Way places on harmony/contentment/peace. The Navajo word for this concept is *hozho*, usually translated as "beauty". But it means far more than beauty, even in the broadest meaning of that word. Attaining *hozho*, regaining it when it is lost, perfecting it, is the ultimate goal of Navajo ceremonialism and the center of Navajo philosophy.

This *hozho* and the lack of it is a central theme in the Navajo version of Genesis.

In that poetic story of how the Navajos came to be, consciousness first existed in a Black World where formless creatures (insects in some versions) discovered themselves alive in a universe of darkness. Details vary considerably among the Navajo clans but in most versions the process of evolution continues through four worlds. In each the *hozho* — essential for the good life — is ruined by disharmony, the world is destroyed, the creatures are forced to flee and eventually emerge in the next world to try again. This new world takes on more shape and detail and so do the creatures. Although two of these individuals are called First Man and First Woman and others have equally specific names of birds and animals, they are not physical beings in the usual sense. They are super-naturals called *Yei* or "Holy People". Again, they are not people but spirits — forces — with supernatural powers, and they are not holy in any ordinary sense of the word. Disharmony among them destroys the Fourth World and they emerge into this Fifth World. In this world, also called Earth Surface World or The Glittering World, the Genesis of the Navajos begins to resemble Greek mythology and the migration story of the Old Testament.

Near Huerfano Mesa southeast of Farmington, New Mexico, the humans who will found the first four Navajo clans are created. Changing Woman, one of the greatest of the Navajo *Yei*, teaches these humans how to live, even to such details as how to build hogans and bake the cake eaten to celebrate a woman's puberty. Changing Woman is impregnated by sunlight and mist from the San Juan River and bears two sons. These become the Navajo Hero Twins. They engage in an odyssey during which the monsters produced by taboo violations in the Fourth World are slain and this world made safe for human occupancy.

But, most important of all, Changing Woman teaches the Navajos the rules to follow to prevent the disharmony which destroyed each of the previous worlds. Then she teaches them how to restore *hozho* if the taboos are violated.

This maintenance of *hozho* is the bedrock of the Navajo Way because Navajo metaphysics is based on a cosmos of precise order. In it, every action has a reaction, nothings happens without cause, and any violation of order produces an inevitable and exactly appropriate retribution.

Living in such a world requires a complicated set of rules to maintain harmony. Violation of these rules causes discordance, which the Navajos relate to sickness, just as health is related to *hozho*. To restore one to *hozho*, the Navajos have an arsenal of ceremonials taught them by Changing Woman and other Holy People. When anthropologists and ethnologists began studying the Navajo religion in the late Nineteenth Century they were able to catalog more than fifty of these ceremonials. While the number still performed today is probably fewer than twenty, their basic purpose has not changed. All of them are intended to restore the cosmic order and to cure the sicknesses caused by taboo violations.

The shaman accomplishes this by reproducing, through the use of sandpaintings and chanted ritual poetry, the proper episodes from Navajo mythology. Different taboo violations require different ceremonies. Some require as long as nine days, some as few as three, and there are medicine people who perform even briefer rituals to deal with minor problems. But the purpose is the same. A taboo has been broken, a rule violated. The harmony of the universe must be restored.

Introduction

I first became acquainted with the Navajos as a small boy
on my grandfather's farm in southern Idaho. In those days
Native Americans were a large part of the migrant labor force
for the same reasons that poor minorities have always done
America's backbreaking grunt labor. Since I was out there
with them, cheek-by-jowl so to speak, the injustice of the situation never occurred to me. Hoeing sugar beets is an indelible
memory of mine, if not a particularly pleasant one. It was just
one of an endless stream of jobs that had to be done, season
by season, on a typically poor, ridiculously small family farm
of the era. In that region of the country sugar beets and the
alienly large brick factories that rendered them into white
crystal sweetness are long gone, as are virtually all the small
farmers who raised them; a couple more victims of
Agribusiness, government meddling, the realities of the
marketplace and changing American tastes.

17

Hoeing sugar beets in Idaho

The work force on this few hundred acres of the American dream consisted of my grandfather, a cousin of mine, and me. Two boys and an old man with occasional help from my mother, who was a top hand. Since all those acres of beets had to be thinned by hand the moment they poked through the soil and then protected from the always rapacious weeds, which seemed much better suited to the soil and climate than the crops, for some reason, we had to have a lot of help in the early Summer. I don't recall any of the Navajos who stayed with us through those Fifties summers waxing philosophical so I can't really say whether they liked the work or not, enjoyed the scenery of Cache Valley, thought the pay was fair, appreciated the house we gave them instead of the tents they got at most places, or particularly cared for my adolescent attentions.

For several years at least, members of the same extended family came each season to help thin and hoe those miserable beets, and although the combination of the uncles and aunts and cousins changed from year to year, there was usually a boy about my age to talk to. I even tried to learn a few words of Navajo way back then. In retrospect, I didn't really learn all that much about Navajos I suppose, but I considered them friends and learned to respect their quiet ways. Because of that early exposure I was interested in learning more, not in the anthropological sense, but because they were friends of my boyhood and seemed wonderfully romantic. The desert Southwest was, and perhaps still is, the last frontier in America.

In 1966, my wife Nannette and I began teaching in the all-Navajo high school at Fort Wingate, New Mexico. At that time the Bureau of Indian Affairs, which had been punishing students for speaking their native language and had vigorously pursued a policy of cultural extermination, was beginning to encourage teachers to use materials which emphasized Navajo culture and I was allowed to develop a series of courses called Southwestern Studies which included literature, history, anthropology, folklore, drama and other subject areas relating to the cultures of the Southwest.

In the winter I told stories I had learned, and with the help of my students I wrote a series of plays based on the Coyote tales which we toured around to schools in the area during the appropriate season.

My actors were all traditionally raised, Navajo speaking kids who were delighted to have the opportunity to draw on their own culture for significant parts of their education and artistic expression — the first generation to be allowed that pleasure. The coyote plays were a big hit.

Later on, when the students learned to trust me and decided my interest was genuine, we began to travel on the Navajo reservation together, attending ceremonies, talking to craftsmen of all kinds, learning the stories and the customs and crafts which many anthropologists already said were dying or dead. It was hard to tell if those academics were happy or sad about that situation, but whichever, they were pretty much wrong. Each generation for the last hundred years or so has predicted the imminent demise of Indian language, culture and the people themselves. The Navajos have managed to thrive in spite of this.

The students realized there was an amazing amount of information about their culture they didn't know, but wanted to learn. In the appropriate seasons we studied these things together. We found many potters and basket weavers and saddle makers besides the better known silversmiths and weavers. The old people were happy that the students and I were interested and kindly shared their knowledge with us. One of the many projects we worked on for four years was the collection of taboos which appears here. All of these taboos came from my students who pretty much represented every area of the reservation.

These taboos reflect the fact that they were collected from and by young people, for many of them deal with the proper behavior of children. There is also a lack of taboos dealing with hunting, warfare, pottery making and a few other things that are now largely part of the past, though I am aware that such taboos did exist and are still known by a few of the old people. Some of these have been collected in the past and are listed in the bibliography.

The taboos found here, then, are those still in general use and circulation. Because the list is long, though certainly not complete, it is impossible to explain the origins of all of them. Many of the taboos are simply examples of common sense, others are indications of the Navajo's awe and respect for nature and natural phenomena. Some have their origins in the sacred myths, legends and tales that are part of the healing ceremonies. The origins of many taboos may be found in Franc Johnson Newcomb's *Navajo Omens and Taboos* . The most detailed explanation of a taboo may be found in Washington Matthews' article "Ichthyophobia."

The taboos are organized here in a way that seemed convenient to me and hopefully this organization does not give any

Snakes are closely related to lightning

false impressions or undue emphasis. The taboos seem to cluster around certain subjects and actions, though a single taboo might rightly fall in more than one category. In the interest of conserving space and giving continuity I have rendered all the taboos in the same format, though they are not always — or even usually — said in this way.

The letter A. indicates the taboo, with variations set off with dashes. The letter B. gives the penalty for violating the taboo, again with variations set off with dashes rather than separate entries. I do not expect all Navajos to agree with any of these taboos, nor any Navajo to recognize all of them. One of the criteria of folklore is that it exists in variations. This is true of all oral traditions. Different medicine men tell even the best-known stories each in his own way. These taboos were collected from hundreds of young Navajos from all parts of the reservation.

The validity of the taboos given here was tested in the classroom. Whenever I received a new taboo I ran it past several classes of my students. If several of them had not heard it before, it was not included. Usually some other student knew a related taboo, or could explain or amplify it. Thus the list grew. The large number of Navajos contributing to this compilation makes it impossible to list their names and a cultural preference for anonymity in cases like this would make such a list a breach of etiquette anyway. We shared what follows among ourselves and now we wish to share it with the reader.

An amusing thing happened many years ago when I was talking about Navajo taboos to a large group of new teachers about to begin teaching on the Navajo reservation. As I spoke, an older man in the audience became increasingly agitated and

annoyed and eventually interrupted me to say, rather petulant-
ly, that the taboos I had been discussing were not Navajo at
all; he had heard almost all of them as a young boy in rural
Oklahoma. I agreed that I had heard some of them in rural
Idaho, Utah and Nevada.

Frankly, most of them can be found in one form or another
all over the world. I could never quite understand why that
universality invalidated them in the mind of the man in that
long-ago audience. His attitude, however, had a lot to do with
the present version of the book, as I refine my approach to
a complicated and delicate subject.

This collection of taboos was assembled more than twenty
years ago now and the original edition was printed by the Navajo Tribe as the first offering in their cultural publications series
from a fairly rough typescript. Ten years later I reprinted the
book using a rough photocopy of the original, adding a bit
of introductory material. I suppose I felt that the material was
self-explanatory to anyone interested enough to read it. I'm
sure now that I was quite mistaken. Over the years I have
had plenty of time to reflect on Navajo culture, this little book,
and the curious ways of mankind in general.

I have also gotten a certain amount of feedback from readers
— Navajo and Anglo alike — and I am amazed at how poorly
the book did the job it was intended to do. It has, in fact, often
accomplished the opposite of what was originally intended —
which was better understanding of taboos specifically and
Navajo culture generally. Way too many readers — many of
them young Navajos — have found the book hilariously funny, curious, peculiar, and proof that Navajos are a simple-
minded folk, riddled by superstition and handicapped by ir-

rational fears and ridiculous perceptions. How in the world did that happen?

So, twenty years after its original publication, *Navajo Taboos* is finally being significantly expanded to include explanations and observations on the taboos themselves, their implications for understanding Navajo culture, some thoughts on Anglo/Navajo relations, and, where possible, the universal nature of a lot of attitudes, fears and superficially curious beliefs.

I am only slightly surprised to find that over the years I have come to honor many of the taboos listed here, whether or not I believe in them literally — and some of them I do, of course. One of the ideas that had become central to my thinking about the body of folk belief represented by these taboos is that literal belief in all or most of them is quite beside the point. Collectively they represent the Navajo soul, the Navajo character, the details by which one Navajo recognizes a fellow member of the tribe in good standing, so to speak.

Many readers have undoubtedly heard that observant orthodox Jews, that is, those closely approximating the Hebrews of the Old Testament have a staggering six hundred and thirteen commandments to observe. In actual fact several hundred of those have to do with temple observance and are thus obsolete and unobserved (at least for the time being). A truly observant Jew has a difficult time in the modern world trying to keep all these commandments, any of which, if broken, violates the Sabbath (Shabos), a mortal sin once punishable by death. Aside from complex dietary laws, rules of dress, ritual washing and prayers, a good Jew may only walk, may not carry, may not light a fire (which includes things like

25

completing an electric circuit — no phone calls, no lights turned on or off) and no work may be done. One of the activities considered work is the act of tearing — even lowly toilet paper — and life is considerably complicated by this. Most of these prohibited things make very little sense to gentiles and a Rabbi might have a hard time explaining some of them in reasonable terms. But they appear in the Torah, are further explicated in the Talmud, or book of laws, and are simply observed. Period. Seems like irrational behavior to an outsider, perhaps, and Jews have paid a great price over the last twenty-five centuries in order to maintain the personal order of their universe and honor their God, who rewards them accordingly.

The real issue here, as with the body of Navajo taboos, is not whether or not all of these complicated observances make sense to outsiders, or even all members of the group, but that, collectively, they give the group its identity which is then passed on to the individual members. An observant Jew is instantly recognizable in any assemblage of people anywhere in the world. He has a very distinct identity and a very deep, ancient, virtually unbreakable link to all of his brothers, no matter what indignities and grief are heaped on him by the outside world. After all these thousands of years the system still seems to be working for them.

Likewise a culturally sensitive Navajo belongs, in effect, to a very exclusive club which, ultimately, will provide him with all of his needs as a human being and which organizes his personal universe in a very definite and distinct way. Another parallel between Judaism and the traditional Navajo Way is the fact that religion cannot be compartmentalized — something only done, or perhaps even thought about, on the

Sabbath. It permeates every thought, every act, every waking moment. Years ago I wanted to tape the autobiography of an elderly Navajo, the grandfather of a student of mine. I chased this old man all over the place; to his summer home in the mountains, to ceremonies, to the homes of relatives. He kept saying — in Navajo of course — that he couldn't tell any sacred stories, especially in the Summertime, as I should well know. Of course not, I assured him, I just want to hear stories of the old days, of your life — nonreligious stories. He would simply look at me in exasperation. I DID eventually realize that to this old man there was no such thing as a secular story, as opposed to a religious story. The storytelling act, itself, was a religious event. I felt pretty foolish when I finally got the point.

Think of the taboos listed in this book (and perhaps hundreds more) as the defining principles of Navajoness — what makes a Navajo a Navajo and not a Hopi, who has a similar, but distinct set of rules to follow. Perhaps much of apparent mental and social illness of the late Twentieth Century is due to the breakdown of a similar set of codified behaviors for the rest of us. Much too complex to get into here, however.

So taboos are not some curious cultural artifact, but rather one of several systems by which correct behavior may be codified and circulated among members of a group. The significant difference between a taboo and any of the other systems mentioned earlier is the notion that violation carries quick and sure punishment and not just censure or punishment in the distant hereafter. It also becomes obvious in looking at the taboos which follow, that the form lends itself to a certain flexibility and creativity. A disgruntled parent, tired of some

For some traditional Navajos Ballroom Dancing could be a form of incest

hyperactive behavior of an offspring, can phrase a prohibition in the form of a taboo and thereby give it more credibility.

No matter how familiar a taboo may sound, no matter how universal the principle it illustrates, there is almost always some specific cultural perspective that makes the Navajo view distinctive from all the others. That same angry redneck I failed to mollify years ago was distressed, for example, by the fact that I suggested that the most important taboo for Navajos was obviously the one prohibiting incest. He observed, with some disgust, that EVERYONE observed the taboo against sleeping with close relatives and that, therefore, it had no significance at all. Not much of a logician, that fellow, but he had a point. What I failed to do was explain just what a traditional Navajo considered to be incestuous behavior — which relationships were involved, which activities, which behaviors. In all fairness, that's where the whole subject gets interesting.

For the record, the oldest, most universal, most abhorred taboos worldwide are incest, cannibalism and patricide, not necessarily in that order. Traditionally these are the first things one culture accuses the neighboring folk of indulging in. Almost all the earliest Europeans to write about the American Indians accused them of all three in a variety of prurient permutations. Home grown pornography disguised as righteous indignation. Even in very ancient times smarter individuals observed that the offspring of close relationships were likely to have too many fingers or too few brain cells. Hence a practical reason for not loving your sister too much. Exogamy had other benefits as well — social, political and economic. But the Navajo outlook on incest is far more extensive and

29

complicated than any other society I have ever read about. Blood relationship isn't even a central criterion. Clan relationship is just as binding as a sibling status, for example. For a traditional Navajo verbal behavior is nearly as significant as the physical act — thus talking dirty to a clan sister would lead to insanity just as quickly as sleeping with a cousin. Living as Navajos traditionally did in great family isolation, but immediate group proximity, put a lot of strain on natural biological urges. Isolated family groups might live miles from the next unrelated family, yet have to share a single dwelling — even a single room — with all the lack of privacy that implies. What a strain. Better make the taboo a strong one.

Thus it comes about that a young Navajo boy is severely disciplined at boarding school because he refuses to dance with a little girl of a different surname selected for him by a well-meaning but culturally insensitive BIA teacher. He simply wasn't able to explain that the girl's grandfather was of the same clan as his great-granny and that even the physical proximity of ballroom dancing compromised an extremely basic taboo. The teacher probably wouldn't have taken it seriously even if it had been explained to her. Too silly.

But that isn't all. Not only is verbal nastiness the same as "going all the way" and not only is a distant clan relationship the same as consanguinity, but certain social relationships come under the taboo umbrella. Female friends of the family of a certain closeness are considered to be clan sisters for purposes of the taboo. On the other hand, when polygamy was still widely practiced, men used to marry sisters simultaneouslyand sometimes a mother and daughter comboand nothing was thought of it. Multiple wives tended to get on better if they

30

were related to each other. Finally, a few very old Navajos still recall the tradition that a boy was not supposed to accept food and other objects directly from the hands of his sister, though this has long since died out as a social behavior. Only a traditionally raised Navajo could possibly understand ALL the implications of this one taboo, so innocently, blandly and nakedly stated in a book of this sort.

It is my intention now to provide a running commentary on as many of the taboos as practical; explaining special circumstances, relating them to other areas of Navajo belief, and dropping an occasional anecdote as the opportunity arises. The things I probably should have done twenty years ago, but didn't think necessary. And that still doesn't begin to exhaust the subject, since I have not felt compelled to put in weeks of research trying to fill in the taboos I knew I missed originally, nor reviewing all the Navajo mythology available (which is extensive) nor even comparing notes with all my Navajo friends to see what they might or might not agree with at this point. This is simply a quarter century of reading, observation and thinking about the subject — presented in a highly personal, probably biased, undoubtedly incomplete and sometimes misleadingly casual way. I must note here that this is the third version of *Navajo Taboos* and the first one to really try to explain the sense of the taboos in Navajo terms, the origin and/or meaning of the taboos, and what makes the universal taboos - like incest - particularly or peculiarly Navajo. In other words, this one-time school project is turning into a real book. I am gratified at the twenty-year success of this modest effort and fully expect to revise the book a few more times, which means that I welcome any suggestions, as well as any corrections, additions or clarifications anyone wishes to address to me at Box 1762, Gallup, New Mexico, 87305. And if Coyote crosses your path, hope he's heading South, with a smile on his face.

TABOO

The word taboo, or tabu, was borrowed from Polynesian and introduced into English by Captain Cook. Taboo is sometimes given specialized meanings in the scholarly literature of anthropology and in the psychology of Sigmund Freud, but in it's most common usage it refers simply to a prohibition.[1] A true taboo, however, has a second component which partially explains why they have become culturally obsolete in so-called sophisticated societies; there is a relatively immediate and unavoidable punishment for violating the taboo.

The paradigm reads something like this: Interdiction + violation = penalty. Unlike moral strictures, the offense is not against God and punishable in the hereafter — the offense is against the natural order and is punishable here and now. Ignorance is no excuse and inadvertently violating a taboo doesn't obviate the punishment in any way.

There are no cultures that do not respect a large number of such prohibitions, though they are often given such labels as rules, laws, mores, folkways and the like. In urban Anglo-American culture taboos are not likely to be verbalized and this leads to the belief that we have no taboos as such. This lack of verbalization involves a major taboo in itself. We do not, for example, willingly or jokingly discuss the imminent possibility of death, mutilation and disease striking ourselves or those close to us.

Such negative social sanctions are, by definition, taboos, especially when accompanied by the belief that such irreverent behavior will cause the thing to happen. I hope I can demonstrate the widespread, if underground, survival of a universal taboo system.

Since the other half of taboo involves the punishment or penalty that results when the taboo is violated, if there is no penalty, there is no taboo. At the very least, the breaking of taboo in Anglo-American society brings the penalty of ridicule, shame or ostracism. In many, if not most societies of the world, the violation of taboo may bring loss of position, social status, wealth, health, and may even result in blindness, madness, crippling disability or, ultimately, death.

In some cases the penalty is immediate and unavoidable; in others it may involve a delay, or the penalty may be transferred to a second party, usually a close member of the family. This transference of penalty is sometimes operational in the Navajo system.

But for Navajos and other Native Americans the fact that the punishment is soon, sudden and unavoidable is most significant. Traditional Navajos had little belief in an after-life and the consequences of "sin" — offenses against the natural order — are punishable in this life, not by future torment, and punishment or its avoidance is not at the whim of some benevolent or malevolent deity. This is reflected rather clearly in a Zuni story called "The Poor Turkey Girl." [2]

The story so remarkably parallels the tale of Cinderella that ethnologists and folklorists refuse to accept an ancient origin for the story, insisting it must have been borrowed from early European contact.

Briefly, the Turkey Girl, like the Ash Boy or "CinderElla", is the lowest of the low. Clad in rags, fed on scraps and despised by the community, this orphan girl herded the domesticated turkeys of the village. She would take them out to feed in the morning, keep them safe from coyotes and other predators and bring them home at night, sleeping with them in their hut. Eventually, through familiar magic, they clothe the girl and send her off to a dance at a neighboring village where she meets and falls in love with a handsome youth. She has now forgotten her promise to be back with her turkey friends by dawn and, when she belatedly arrives home, the turkeys are gone and she eventually dies in disgrace.

The full story is so remarkably like the European tale it is uncanny, but the significant difference — the ending — seems much too important to me to simply be an alteration of a borrowed story. Repeatedly in Native American mythology (and there are a number of familiar, European-sounding stories and motifs, especially in the Creation myths) the Indian version of reality results in the heroes being punished for their failings, misdeeds or shortcomings, unlike their Anglo counterparts. The individual is accountable for his own actions and the punishment is swift, inevitable and final.

The few taboo-like structures that come easily to mind for the average Anglo-American — those involving black cats, ladders, broken mirrors or spilt salt — are usually thought of as superstitions and not taken seriously. Because of our prohibition against talking about certain subjects, the real taboos are seldom articulated, except for the obvious — like the Ten Commandments, for example; and even here the punishment is vague and delayed — but we observe a huge number of

35

The Zuni Turkey Girl

taboos nonetheless.

Most people of the world are ethnocentric, believing that their own culture is correct and all other cultures incorrect to the degree that they differ from one's own. This is, of course, a natural thing. A culture which is not to some degree ethnocentric would soon be absorbed by another culture with more faith in itself. But this attitude is also blinding and produces a great deal of strife and misunderstanding. It gives humans the tendency to look for differences rather than similarities in their fellow human beings. I have heard many Anglo-Americans laugh at the sacred Navajo stories, calling them pagan or heathen, labelling them myths in the sense of untruths.

All of this in spite of the fact that the sacred stories of the Navajos have a great many parallels in the Bible. Few Anglo-Americans like to hear the Bible stories referred to as myths, though they differ in content and meaning very little from similar religious tales found all over the world.

The same is true of many of the taboos which follow here. Franc Johnson Newcomb, author of a number of books on the Navajos, has called the taboos "odd bits of folklore" and "superstitions," and seems to apologize for those who are still unsophisticated enough to believe in them. She also apologizes to the reader saying that "some of these may sound foolish or childish." [3] I make no such apology. None of the taboos which follow seem to me to be either foolish or childish. If the reader will reflect seriously on the taboos he will see the common sense and logic underlying them. Those which seem most strange to an Anglo-American are the taboos involving sympathetic magic, or magic by association — which has an evil

37

side in the widespread belief and practice of witchcraft. Sympathetic magic is based on the view that the part reconstructs the whole, that an object or action symbolically represents or reconstructs a related object or action. Like produces like. A bear claw necklace, an eagle feather bonnet, a mountain lion skin quiver, all give their possessor some measure of the characteristics of those animals — strength, cunning, ferocity, the ability to soar.

This same "power by association" motivates some autograph collectors. A plastic representation of Jesus on the dashboard of a car in a like way is felt to attract His special protection. Modern dream theories applied in psychoanalysis also reflect the principles of sympathetic magic. Looked at this way, it is easy to see why Navajos associate snakes with lightning, salt with white hair, and eclipses with blindness.

The usual definition of sympathetic magic — stated here as "Like produces like" — appears to me to include the fact that sympathetic magic often works, on a psychological if not physical level. Somehow this part of the formula seems to get forgotten. Further, sympathetic magic requires more than "eye of newt, and toe of frog, wool of bat, and tongue of dog" to have any real validity. Preliterate cultures — socalled "primitive' peoples — may be relatively simple, but they are not stupid.

Sympathetic magic draws on a codified body of beliefs, a significant population of believers and a tradition of long standing. In other words, the formulas are specific, the belief in their power is generally attested to by the population at large, and the proof is in the longevity of the tradition. Anything less is not sympathetic magic, but wishful thinking.

For the record, more than a dozen of the taboos that follow, including several relating to snakes, may be found in Mark Twain's classic *Huckleberry Finn*.[4] He attributes most of them to Negro folklore of the old South, but, in fact, they were commonly held beliefs by most rural folk of whatever color. Most of the Uncle Remus stories, by the way, were Native American in origin, not African, which doesn't have anything to do with taboos, but is interesting, nonetheless.

There is no Navajo word for taboo, though Grenville Goodwin gives the word *gudnlsi* in his book *Western Apache Raiding and Warfare*.[5] The Navajo word *bahadzid* meaning it is feared or injurious, dangerous, is most often used in connection with taboos. This is related to *baahadzidii*, poison, and *baahagii*, sin, crime or misdeed.[6] When Franz Steiner, in *Taboo*, says, "One might say that taboo deals with the sociology of danger itself," he is expressing the Navajo view exactly.[7] Taboos are prescriptions of proper behavior, ESPECIALLY in dangerous or potentially dangerous situations.

The Navajo country imposes on its residents the obligation of independence and self-reliance, conditions which shaped Anglo-American character in the days of the frontier. Though there is an excellent Navajo police force and the Public Health Service has provided several hospitals in the Reservation area, most Navajos sill live far from the immediate protection of society.

If a hogan catches fire it simply burns down; there is no nearby fire station, and no water anyway. A sick Navajo may have to travel more than a hundred miles to the nearest doctor or hospital, most of those miles over unimproved roads

Navajos avoid looking into mirrors at night

which may be impassable after a heavy rain or a snow storm. The Navajo police cannot be expected to patrol every part of the thousands of square miles of wild country that makes up Navajoland. In such a situation prevention is more important than cure. Without the protective agencies that urban Anglo-Americans can reach quickly with a shout or a phone call, the Navajo must protect himself.

The major part of this protection comes from knowing the correct behavior in any dangerous situation. The taboos indicate appropriate behavior — though stated negatively. Most Navajo taboos have several underlying rationalizations or strata of explanation, especially the more important or universal ones. On the obvious level there is usually a physical or practical component that is readily accessible. For example: The prohibition against drinking directly from the mouth of a spring would keep a precious resource from being contaminated — or even worse, destroyed by a rockslide or similar disaster. On the philosophical level a good Navajo would not be careless nor greedy and would show good manners by drinking a little downstream. But on a really spiritual level, where magic, religion and the supernatural powers are effective, the prohibition is more likely an oblique reference to the significance of a person's reflection.

Almost all early peoples believed that a shadow or reflection of an individual was a manifestation of his very soul and shouldn't be separated from the person. Hence the early fear of photography. There was a widespread belief that the camera, or the photo itself, captured a person's soul. Photographers were referred to as "shadow catchers" by many Native American peoples.

Mythology, folklore and literature are full of such references to the power of reflected images: Think of *The Picture of Dorian Gray*, for example, or the inability of vampires to cast a reflection. One of the small handful of Anglo sayings which follows the taboo formula his the bad luck prohibition of breaking a mirror — obviously a vestigial remnant of a more serious belief now otherwise lost in antiquity. Magical mirrors are a ubiquitous component of fairy tales from Snow White to King Arthur to *Alice Through the Looking Glass*. In this vein, the "mouth" of a spring often forms a still pool which would have potent magical reflecting properties.

Finally, most taboos, as stated, reflect proper behavior which would automatically be adhered to by right-thinking, upstanding members of the culture, whether they subscribed to the underlying explanation or not. One need not believe that saying the word "bear" in Navajo would actually draw attention from one of the creatures, as the taboo states. A Navajo would try to avoid saying it and causing discomfort to other members of the group who did believe.

Likewise, a Navajo may not believe that wearing a ring on the thumb or forefinger made him a witch, but he wouldn't be caught dead doing it all the same. Why draw unnecessary negative attention from peers?

People living the relatively simple life of a non-technological society, close to the land, will recognize the validity of much that the city dweller is insulated from by his machines and likes to dismiss as superstition. It is encouraging that today many people are rediscovering these truths, and in America, the Indians have been the major preservers of this sometimes more sensitive way of life with its emphasis on concern for the feelings of others and the rights of the animals and environment of the natural world. Of course, in this day and age, many Navajos have long since abandoned this aspect of traditional life as pure superstition, much to their loss.[8]

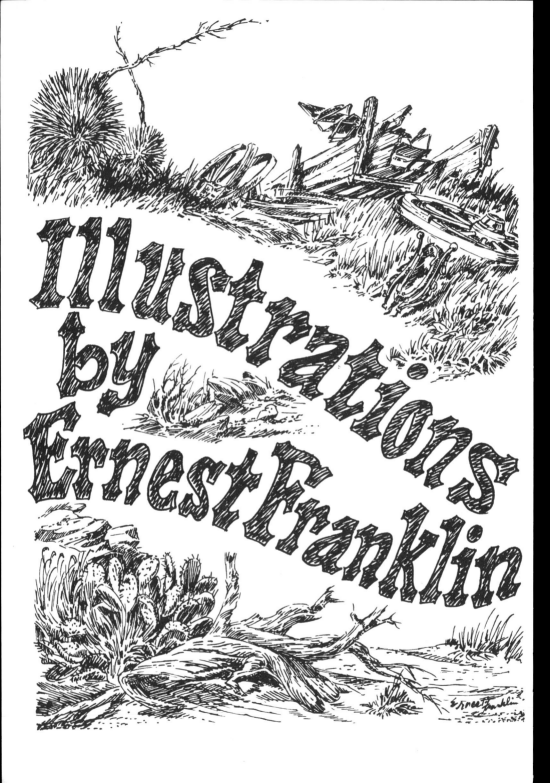

THE ILLUSTRATIONS

Ernest Franklin, my friend of twenty-five years, sometimes advisor, collaborator and favorite illustrator, has contributed a new color cover and fifty illustrations for this new edition of *Navajo Taboos*. He is a full-blooded Navajo from the Twin Lakes area who spoke only Navajo until he was carted off to boarding school as a boy.

He has spent his lifetime around horses and livestock, branding and shearing, rodeos and traditional ceremonies of healing. He has spent his share of time hauling firewood and herding sheep, looking for lost livestock and watching the wind blow, repairing saddles and getting pickups unstuck from the southwestern gumbo during the short rainy season, all traditional activities for a Reservation Navajo. And always there was his art.

He drew from an early age, often on paper sacks and other found materials, though he was never encouraged to think of art as a life's work — as legitimate employment. After various government schools and a stint in Vietnam he gravitated toward the Job Corps, the Bureau of Indian Affairs and the Navajo Tribe as a way to make a living and stay on or near the Reservation — the only acceptable place for a real Navajo to live. For many years he taught art to young Navajos at Wingate High School in Fort Wingate, New Mexico, the place where Navajos first met the invading Anglos.

For years he played country music in a small band, drew caricatures of retiring government employees for retirement parties and tried his hand at silversmithing, leatherwork, woodcarving and about any art form that caught his attention.

And all the time he kept drawing working cowboys, his subject of choice. Franklin's artistic influences have mostly been the masters of Western art, Remington, Russell and the boys, who have only been accepted as fine artists themselves in fairly recent years. Ernie is mostly self-taught and has explored almost every possible medium at some time or another. These days he specializes in watercolor, a most difficult and demanding medium.

Over the years he has won many ribbons and awards at Gallup Ceremonial, the New Mexico State Fair and the Navajo Tribal Fair. He has also had a number of one-man exhibits in the Gallup area. Recently he has become the official illustrator of the Navajo detective stories by bestseller Tony Hillerman and his illustrations have appeared in books, magazines and catalogs.

Anyone familiar with Navajo culture will immediately recognize the validity and appropriateness of Franklin's lighthearted approach to a subject which delineates the Tribe's deepest fears, least tolerated behaviors, and most awesome dangers.

The Coyote Stories long since established humor, mockery of excessive behavior, and a culture hero who embodies all of society's worst characteristics as a viable way of presenting moral lessons to its members. The Coyote Tales are ribald, violent stories of wretched excess, stupidity and improper behavior which use humor and exaggeration to make their points. I know of no group of people who have more fun with life than the traditional Navajos who are great teasers and practical jokers and who delight in complex verbal puns. This is the tradition Ernie Franklin has drawn on for his illustrations.

THE TABOOS

COYOTE THE TRICKSTER

Coyote is the most wonderful, and contradictory, figure in Navajo life and mythology. Coyote, the ultimate trickster figure, is as much god as joker, as much creator as evil spirit. His excessive behavior is the model of anti-social behavior and yet he is a central figure in Navajo mythology. He is bisexual, virtually unkillable because of his ability to hide his life force, he is enigmatic, powerful, contradictory, all-encompassing — everything and nothing at the same time. For many of the Native American groups in the Southwest the keepers — policemen if you will — of culture are also the clowns, which may seem contradictory to many Anglos. The mudheads, koshares and other clown fraternities have a deadly serious purpose behind their raucous, usually sexually vulgar, always exaggerated and often violent antics as they remind the people how easy it is to overstep the boundaries of proper behavior. Coyote functions in much the same way — representing the model of improper behavior and keeping order by ridiculing and satirizing all sorts of outrageous, destructive behaviors. Native Americans in general have a great sense of humor and love to play practical jokes on one another, mocking the conventions of society which tend to be rather confining in small-group dynamics. Some Pueblo villages are so small now that everyone not only knows everyone else, and knows their business, but they are all related by blood. There is a

51

great deal of pressure for conformity in such a group, as dramatized in Frank Waters' Taos Pueblo novel *The Man Who Killed The Deer*.

Though the Navajo population is much larger, and scattered over hundreds of square miles of territory, the tribal unit known as the "Chapter" functions much like any small community and a good sense of humor is an invaluable escape valve for the pressures of day-to-day life when dealing with a limited peer group. Put it this way — when everyone in your immediate world is your in-law, it pays to have a sense of humor. While the taboos themselves are a paradigm of "proper" behavior, the Coyote character, in a virtually endless round of adventures told in story form, routinely violates and mocks these underpinnings of society, much to the delight of Navajo audiences when the stories are told.

While Coyote is centrally important in traditional Navajo life, he is the object of almost no taboos — perhaps because of his role as violator of custom, flaunter of respectable behavior. All the same, he always seems to be lurking out there, just out of sight, a shadowy figure who can be as fearsome as he is funny.

The single Coyote taboo which comes readily to mind isn't exactly a proper taboo in form at all:

A. If Coyote crosses your path, turn back and do not continue your journey.

B. Something terrible will happen to you — you will have an accident — be hurt or killed.

The Coyote part of this taboo really functions as an omen. The taboo is against ignoring the warning delivered by the appearance of Coyote. As it turns out, there are a lot of refinements attached to this taboo, and at least a couple of available escape routes, so to speak. Virtually every traditional Navajo has a fund of Coyote anecdotes in which the warning was ignored, or at least not taken seriously enough, and something bad happened as a result. I have a few coyote anecdotes of my own.

One of the first times I encountered the taboo was more than twenty-five years ago on a bitterly cold night, in a snowstorm, approaching midnight. Several Navajo students and I were almost to our destination in a remote part of the Reservation when a large coyote crossed in the headlights. Since I knew the taboo and my passengers were traditionals, I stopped the car to talk over the situation. It was pretty ridiculous to backtrack under the circumstances, though I didn't want to appear insensitive to local belief. We finally decided to continue — less than a mile as it turned out — to the home of one of the boys. He immediately told his grandmother what happened and she seemed quite concerned. Then she asked if the coyote had been going from left to right or vice versa. Right to left, we said. With a sigh of relief she said everything was o.k., but to be careful for a day or two. It turns out that right and left had nothing to do with the situation, per se, but the fact that the coyote had been travelling South, which is much better than North, which is the direction of evil spirits, darkness and general bad luck. There is a complex of beliefs concerning the direction of travel of the coyote, the people involved, the ultimate destination of either one and so on.

On another occasion I was riding with a young Navajo in a pickup when a dog coyote crossed our path, trotting brazenly along in broad daylight. My friend slammed on the brakes, grabbed a rifle from the rack in the back window, jumped out of the truck and shot the coyote dead. He grabbed it by the tail and dragged it back over its own tracks until he had it on the other side of the road we were following, then got back in the truck and drove on. The bad luck had apparently been canceled.

Less dramatically, I know of a mini-ceremony which can be performed over the coyote tracks to break the spell when the trip is simply too important to be abandoned. It involves pollen, small offerings of turquoise and the breaking of the tracks, but should only be performed when absolutely necessary. And, of course, nothing works perfectly all the time.

Generally, Coyote is avoided whenever possible. Most Navajos say it is taboo to kill a coyote, while routinely killing them in defense of their sheep, for example. On the whole, Coyote is taboo in the same way that other "bad" animals are in their negative influence on pregnant women, for example. Just for the record, here is the only Coyote taboo from the original list:

A. Don't bother a coyote that takes the first-born goat or lamb.

B. It is his — keeps order in the world. If he is given the first-born freely, he hopefully will leave the rest in peace.

This is a clear acknowledgement of Coyote's role as a creator figure and to his importance in the Navajo cosmology. Just don't forget that he's always out there waiting.

NATURE AND NATURAL POWERS

A. Don't point at a rainbow with your finger.
B. It will cut it off — break your fingers.

It is improper behavior to point at anyone or anything with the extended forefinger, probably because of the threatening connotations of the gesture. Navajos point with pursed lips, a sort of kissing gesture which Anglos often find disconcerting at first, and then generally pick up themselves if they stay around long enough. And, of course, the symbolic nature of the rainbow as a manifestation of life-giving rain is universal.

In the Bible, the first of the great covenants between God and man was signed, sealed and delivered with the multi-colored sky bridge and in the desert Southwest a good rainbow can be a breathtaking sight. Rainbows appear regularly in Navajo sandpaintings and, like anything to do with water, have strong religious significance.

A. Don't throw rocks at a whirlwind.
B. It will throw them back — chase you.

A. Don't call a whirlwind names.
B. Evil spirits will get you.

A. Don't go into a whirlwind.
B. It will affect your heart — carry you off.

Dust devils are in ill wind that blows no-one any good and seem to be animated by evil spirits. I have been told by Navajos

57

Don't point at a rainbow

that one can speak to these whirling winds to beg their indulgence and they may be jokingly referred to as "brother-in-law" which is a slightly bawdy relationship by tradition.

Winds have great religious significance for Navajos and many other people as the source of life and breath.[9] In some Native American languages the words for air, breath, speech and soul clearly derive from the same root.

A. Don't whistle too loud, or four days in a row.
B. You'll call up the wind.

Whistling is discouraged in several contexts as will be seen elsewhere, but a Finn told me once that Scandinavians had a similar taboo. I'm sure it is found in other places as well.

A. Don't stand on high rocks.
B. They will grow into the sky with you.

A. Don't roll a rock from the mountain.
B. The Holy People put them there — bad luck.

Virtually every high spot on the Reservation and every unusual rock formation has religious significance, holiness.[10] Throughout history most Gods have resided on mountain peaks, or chosen mountaintops as an appropriate meeting place between God and mortal. Pueblo Kachinas and Navajo Yeis, in time honored fashion, have favored the high ground as well. Priests who wish to commune with these mystical powers must climb, and offerings are often an important part of the process. Thus the uninitiated are often discouraged from loitering in such places. In several Navajo myths heroes were taken into the sky home of the Holy People by the device of being carried upward by high rock formations.

A. Don't look at clouds moving in the sky.
B. You'll be a slow runner.

A. Don't watch a river flowing swiftly.
B. You'll get dizzy and fall in.

These two, and to some extent the taboo which follows, il-lustrate a basic tenet of Navajo life — laziness is ugly and un-Navajo and daydreaming is not encouraged.

A. Don't stare at the moon.
B. It will follow you.

Whatever the practical reasons, almost all peoples through time have made the association between moonlight and madness — hence the word "lunatic." Navajos, however, have an exaggerated avoidance of darkness and things of the night — at least in part because the prevalence of witchcraft and the dark arts. The Navajos also seem to find lunar eclipses more significant and frightening than solar ones. There are whispered stories of human sacrifices to bring the moon back to life.[11]

This taboo doesn't refer to a literal interference of heaven-ly bodies, but the fact that idling about in the darkness is likely to attract unhealthy and unwanted attention. I am surprised that there are not more moon taboos in the collection.

A. Don't eat when there is an eclipse.
B. You will have a swollen stomach — stomach trouble

A. Don't sleep during the eclipse.
B. Your eyes won't open again.

A. Don't look at an eclipse.
B. You'll go blind.

The "death" of the sun, as of the moon, is a fearful and ominous thing and often called for great sacrifices. The Aztecs had a complex set of beliefs on the subject. Blindness is, of course, the literal punishment for staring at the sun with the naked eye.

A. Don't look at a shooting star unless you blow at it.
B. You'll have trouble — bad luck.

A. Don't look at a falling star.
B. You'll get bad news.

Shooting star and falling star are logically the same thing, of course and I know of several formulas by which such sightings are omens of GOOD luck, rather than bad. Again, much of traditional Navajo lore dealing with things of the night seems to be frightening and pessimistic. Perhaps this is why Navajo ceremonies tend to last until dawn and sunup, when travel would be safer. The significant thing here is the mention of a countermeasure to avoid the inevitable bad consequence of violating a taboo. This one would only be violated inadvertently anyhow. As mentioned elsewhere in this study, there ARE sometimes things (other than expensive ceremonies) which can counter bad omens.

A. Don't catch snow when it is falling.
B. It will keep on falling — get deep.

A. Don't hold out your hands when it is snowing.
B. Where your hand is, is how deep the snow will be.

A. Don't eat the first snow.
B. It will make you sick.

A. Don't shake a flour sack in the winter.
B. The snow will get big — cause blizzards.

A. Don't start a fire with a magnifying glass.
B. You'll have a burning in your stomach.

A. Don't walk along the track of rainwater.
B. You'll catch cold — make more rain — cause a flood.

We find many references to "tracks" and "footprints" in
Navajo culture, especially in the mythology and taboo lore.
Fingerprints are the tracks of the Holy Winds that breathed
life into First Man and First Woman. Footprints retain enough
of the individual who made them to be used in witchcraft —
especially those of small children. There is a general avoidance
of prints left by bears, snakes and other dangerous animals.
While "tracks" of rainwater are more subtle than those of
animals, they are certainly not less powerful. What is referred to here are the winding ribbon-like marks at the bottom
of arroyos, canyons, washes and other watercourses which
carry the runoff of thunderstorms. The importance and
religious significance of rain comes up repeatedly in Navajo
lore and water is so precious in the desert that even the marks
of its passing are powerful. Sand piled up by the action of
rainwater is also generally avoided for any sort of household
application. This taboo is consistent with avoiding any
disrespect to the rain spirits.

A. Don't bathe in rainwater or a lake formed by rain (girls).
B. The male rain will mate with you.

Changing Woman was made pregnant by water (or rainwater) to conceive the younger of the Hero Twins. The taboo
specifically refers to a temporary puddle formed by a storm,
not a permanent lake or river. It is somewhat related to the
taboo above.

It's not a good idea to sleep while herding sheep

PINON NUTS

Since the nut of the pinon pine was a staple food in the rather limited Navajo larder until recent years and still provides a cash crop for many Navajos in the fall, it is not surprising that there are a number of taboos relating to the resinous nuts and their gathering. Before the Navajos came into the Southwest and learned corn agriculture from the Pueblos there were undoubtedly many more taboos associated with the handling of this natural food. The pinon tree is found over a great area of the American west and was vital to many tribes, especially in the Great Basin.

A. Don't sleep on a pinon shell.
B. It will go into you — you aren't showing respect.

This also implies that the person is untidy and lazy to leave discarded shells in the bedding. There are other taboos against eating in bed as well.

A. Don't shake a pinon tree to get the nuts.
B. Only bears do that.

Behaving like a bear implies uncouth, unrestrained behavior besides attracting them to the individual. There are several related taboos in the category "Animals".

A. Don't eat the nuts from a lightning struck pinon.
B. You'll swell up — have bad luck.

A crossover taboo where the lightning aspect is perhaps more important than the pinon. Some believe that such a tree has

Salting pinon nuts makes it snow

been taken by the spirits and any nuts it produces are their property.

A. Don't put salt on pinons.
B. It will make it snow.

A. Don't burn pinon shells.
B. The snow will be deep.

A. Don't throw pinon shells in water.
B. It will be very cold.

A. Don't wash your hair when you are picking pinons.
B. It will get cold and there will be no more nuts.

Like the first taboo in this series, these activities imply lack of respect for an important natural food. There is a limited time the nuts can be easily harvested in the fall and an intelligent Navajo doesn't waste time in frivolous activities like hair washing when there is important work to be done.

LIGHTNING

The large number of taboos associated with lightning can only be really understood by those who have lived in the Southwest. Though lightning is everywhere one of the most powerful effects in Nature's bag of tricks, in the Southwest it is even more awesome and terrible. Lightning is the major cause of forest fires and kills large number of livestock and people every year. In a single year in the late Sixties I knew six people struck by lighting — three of them fatally. A teacher at the school was knocked to the ground and lost several teeth within a few feet of the front door. One of my students was hauling water with her mother when the wagon they were using got stuck in the sand. She got down to urge the horses and a lightning bolt killed her mother, still on the wagon, and badly injured both horses.

Another student was herding sheep with her little brother when a flash flood threatened. She couldn't handle the sheep and take care of the small boy at the same time so she put him under an overhanging cliff where he would be safe from the storm. Before she was out of sight down the canyon lighting struck the cliff four times and a huge chunk of rock killed the child. Bizarre happenings involving lightning are common on the Reservation and most everyone has a good lightning story — if not several.

The Southwest mocks the proverb that lightning never strikes twice in the same place; here, it almost always strikes repeatedly. Trees and rocks that are regularly struck by lightning often

Lightning is unusually powerful in the Southwest

have ceremonial significance to the Navajos, though only a qualified medicine man will touch, remove or otherwise bother with such objects. "Talking rock medicine" is partly compounded from cave rock that has been repeatedly struck by lightning. While traveling north of Pinon, Arizona, I once saw lightning strike from a completely cloudless sky. Though a meteorologist would explain that dust particles in the sky could generate an electrical charge just the same as water molecules, it is still an unusual and disconcerting sight and smacks of the supernatural.

A. Don't use partly burned wood.
B. It might be from a lightning struck tree — cause illness or bad luck.

A. Don't stand up when there is lightning.
B. If you sit down it will go away.

A. Don't yell when it is raining.
B. You'll be struck by lightning.

A. Don't have a dog or cat in the hogan during a storm.
B. It will draw the lightning.

Most everyone has gotten static electricity from petting a cat, so the connection here is obvious. Less obvious is the fact that domestic animals are not much indulged by Navajos and are seldom pampered. They are more likely to be seen as dangerous, as are most wild animals.

They are not considered members of the family and anthropomorphesized as many Anglos are wont to do. Other taboos involving dogs and cats are scattered throughout the categories.

A. Don't look at lightning in a mirror.
B. It will strike you or your hogan.

Here is another mirror reference which illustrates the magical — and sometimes evil — properties they contain.

A. Don't kill a nighthawk.
B. You'll be struck by lightning.

I don't know why the nighthawk is associated with lightning except that it is very quick. The nighthawk, or bull bat, is the bird often seen flying around street lights in the late evening and mistaken for a bat as it swoops and flutters silently for insects attracted to the light. In Navajo lore the nighthawk is associated with rain.

At night in the Sonoran Desert, I have heard them make an eerie purring sound something like a motorcycle far off in the distance — perhaps like the distant rumble of thunder.

A. Don't use aspen wood for a fire.
B. It causes thunder and lightning.

In the mountain country of New Mexico the Hispanic population uses a lot of aspen for firewood but it is very soft and burns up quickly. Since some Navajos have to haul their firewood a long distance it may as well be the better burning pinon or cedar they prefer. Aspen is, however, said to reduce the creosote buildup in stovepipes and chimneys.

A. Don't eat nuts from a lightning struck pinon tree.
B. You'll swell up — get sick — have bad luck.

A. Don't stand by the loom when it is raining.
B. The lightning will strike you.

72

A. Don't weave when it is storming.

B. It will cause lightning — depending on the pattern.

There is, of course, the famous storm pattern rug of the Eastern Reservation, a design with many lightning motifs. Zigzag patterns are common in many rug designs, however, and are considered to be representations of lightning. The important idea here is that the act of creation — rug or whatever — is a magical and powerful thing in itself. There are a great many taboos associated with weaving and even more with pottery making.

A. Don't climb a tree when it is raining.

B. Lightning might strike that tree.

A. Don't lean against the wall during a storm.

B. The lightning will strike you.

A. Don't ride a horse during a storm.

B. You'll be struck by lightning.

A. Don't touch metal objects when it is raining.

B. You'll get electrocuted by the lightning.

A. Don't wash your hair when it is raining.

B. You'll be struck by lightning.

A. Don't eat an animal killed by lightning.

B. You'll be struck by lightning — get sick.

A. Don't play around a lightning struck tree.

B. You'll get sick.

A. Don't call the thunder's name.

B. The lightning will get you.

Another of the taboos which illustrates the power of the

Dogs and cats are cast adrift in a lightning storm

spoken word, names, and a general reverence for natural phenomena.

A. Don't do a rain dance during a rain storm.
B. You'll be struck by lightning.

A. Don't lay facing the sky in a storm.
B. The lightning will strike you.

A. Don't eat corn when it is raining.
B. Lightning will strike you.

The first half of this series is common sense, and can be found all over the world. Everyone with any sense knows to stay away from trees in a thunderstorm. The second half of the series has more to do with the religious attitudes - dancing for rain when it is already storming would certainly be seen as sacrilegious, a mocking of the gods. I'm uncertain about the final one, but corn plants and ears of corn have a lot of ritual significance and offerings of cornmeal and corn pollen are part of every ceremony I know of in the Southwest, so corn would be attractive to the Lightning People. Most of these taboos share the common thread of being respectful of natural powers.

WILD ANIMALS

It is interesting that few wild animals or birds are considered friendly to the Navajos. Owls, crows, mice and coyotes are considered helpers of the witches and evil spirits and are mentioned as such in the mythology. When the monsters were seeking the infant Hero Twins, for example, the above mentioned animals spied for them. Cottontail rabbits are also associated with witches. While bear claws are commonly worn for their talismanic power by almost all Native Americans, Navajo avoid any part of such animals. Antlers from elk and deer are not used, though mountain sheep horn, buffalo parts and antelope horn are all used ritually. Navajos may use mountain lion skin and a few feathers, notably eagle. Most others are prohibited.

All water animals are the subject of taboo; undoubtedly because they indicate the presence of sweet, fresh water in a country where a tiny catch pool in the rocks may mean life or death to the traveler, especially back in the days of foot and horseback travel. Snakes are associated with lightning and rain and the large number of snake taboos are included in a separate category. Avoidance of animals, especially "bad" animals, is a huge category of pregnancy taboos. Dead animals are even more powerful in their ability to cause harm to children and expectant women and unborn babies.

A. Don't kill frogs (lizards, salamanders, toads).

B. It will rain and keep on raining — cause a flood — ruin your crops — you'll jump around — become crippled — affect your unborn child — cause paralysis & other diseases.

Ernest Franklin

This is one of those taboos that seems silly to some Anglos and used to cause a lot of grief in government schools where biology teachers expected Navajo kids to dissect frogs or other aquatic animals. Actually a Navajo has no business fooling with any dead animal — but especially not the ones associated with water.

A. Don't kill horned toads.

B. They are grandfathers — guardians of arrowheads — You'll get a stomach ache — swell up — have a heart attack.

Related to the one above, this taboo deals with a desert lizard which figures largely in Navajo mythology. In the Hero Twins story, Horny Toad gives Slayer of Enemy Gods the spines from his head and back which turn into deadly arrows used to kill one of the largest and most fearful monsters — hence the association with arrowheads, which are the only old objects that can be picked up by a Navajo from Anasazi ruins.

In one of the Coyote tales Horny Toad is swallowed by Coyote and kills him by cutting an X on his heart. If a Navajo encounters a horny toad he may pick him up, stroke him gently and call him "grandfather" and good luck will come.

A. Don't watch a frog eat.

B. You'll have throat problems later — trouble swallowing.

A. Don't kill a spider unless you draw a circle around it and say, "you have no relatives," or "a Zuni did it."

B. It's relatives will come and bite you.

Some people say the same about snakes and this notion is

Navajos avoid all animals associated with water

used by Mark Twain in *Huckleberry Finn*. Many cultures have prohibitions against killing spiders, especially inside a house. For most Native American groups saying "you have no relatives" is a terrible insult. In this case it also means they aren't invited around. The reason for blaming the deed on a Zuni should be obvious, the angry arachnids will look for a Zuni to bite.

A. Don't urinate on an ant hill.
B. You'll have trouble going to the bathroom.

A. Don't burn ants.
B. Red spots will appear on your body — rash.

Ants feature importantly in Navajo mythology, notably in "The Red Ant Way Ceremony" and they have supernatural powers. There are several taboos concerning urinating on, or in front of, various animals probably stemming from the fact that it is a biological function involving fluid on the one hand, and a sexual connotation on the other.

A. Don't burn bees.
B. You'll have a rash.

A. Don't throw stink bugs in the fire.
B. You'll get a rash — sores.

A. Don't kill grasshoppers.
B. It will give you a nosebleed.

I always heard they spit tobacco juice on you but the connection is obviously the brown spit they seem to come up with when hurt. But bees, grasshoppers, cicadas and many other insects are important in the Creation story and elsewhere in Navajo mythology and all living things, even flies, have their place in the natural order.

A. Don't bother baby hawks or eagles.
B. You'll get a rash or sores on your body.

A. Don't kill moths.
B. You'll jump in the fire.

A. Don't count the number of legs on a centipede.
B. The number you count will be the number of years you have left to live.

A. Don't kill a bald headed insect and spider.
B. You'll go bald.

A. Never carry crow feathers (owl, buzzard, almost any bird but eagle).
B. You'll get boils.

This is an almost perfect series of taboos involving sympathetic magic, as explained above. The connections here between deed and punishment are all pretty obvious.

A. Don't kill porcupines.
B. You'll have nosebleeds.

Porcupine's connection to nosebleeds comes from a Coyote tale known as "The Bungling Host" and found, in variants, all over the world. Coyote tries to mimic Porcupine's magic with predictably poor results.

A. Don't spit on a spider web.
B. You won't be able to breathe right.

A. Don't put food in a bird's mouth.
B. You will have a sore throat.

Blame dead spiders on somebody else

A. Don't kill a lizard.
B. You'll get skinny.

A. Don't burn any animal skin.
B. You'll get a rash.

A. Don't urinate on a deerskin.
B. You'll clog up.

A. Don't have sex with animals.
B. You'll die — go crazy.

Moths are associated with crazy behavior and fire

SNAKES

To discuss the significance of snakes in any detail would require a separate publication. The well-known plumed serpent of the Aztecs may be found in some form throughout the Americas and is clearly represented in the ceremonial life of the Hopis and Zunis, close neighbors of the Navajos. The snake, like the coyote, has a dual nature, having both good and evil characteristics. The poisonous snakes of the Southwest pose a real threat to both livestock and humans, but the snake is also a representation of the lightning people and brings rain to the arid land. Snakes are represented in many Navajo sand-paintings, and the taboos which follow here barely touch on the significance of the snake in Indian life.

A. Don't cross a snake's path unless you slide or shuffle your feet.

B. You'll have leg aches — other diseases — bad luck.

A. Don't eat in front of a snake.

B. When you get older, your throat will close.

A. Don't watch a snake swallow it's food.

B. Your neck will swell up.

A. Don't watch a water snake swallow.

B. You'll lose your voice.

Holding things between your first two fingers is acting like a snake

In a way, snakes seem to be all throat, after all. Many kinds can unhinge their jaws in order to swallow prey larger than their own heads. Together, these attributes suggest things to do with throat, neck and vocal chords combined with the general taboo against staring and the special powers of the serpent family.

A. Don't open your mouth when you see a snake.
B. He'll jump in.

Just another way of saying "don't be a dunce."

A. Don't kill snakes or lizards.
B. It will make your heart small — dry up — you will get a crooked back.

A. Don't burn a snake.
B. You'll get sores — rash.

A. Don't kill a snake when it is raining.
B. Lightning will strike your house.

A. Don't put a snake in the open when dead.
B. The lightning will bring it back to life.

A. Don't put a dead snake on a rock.
B. You'll cause a thunderstorm — it will come back to life.

Remember that snakes are the earthly manifestation of the Lightning People and related to the Thunders and are in communication with these supernaturals. Exposing dead snakes to the sky will draw attention from the Serpent Spirits. Wantonly killing snakes will drive away the life-giving rains and cause a drought.

A. Don't kill a snake with your hand.
B. Your hand will swell up.

A. Don't go to the bathroom in front of a snake.
B. He will be jealous of your wife and turn her yellow.

This is one of those taboos which picks up on several different elements. There is a sort of joke about the resemblance between a snake and a male sex organ for a start. Then a sort of explanation for jaundice or liver disease, though I'm not sure how seriously that is meant to be taken. All together this is another of those taboos that is more euphemism than literal truth. The sense of it is that one should be circumspect about biological functions and considerate of the natural world.

A. Don't pick up things between two fingers.
B. Only snakes do that.

This is really a reference to the forked tongue of a snake, obviously, and the scissorlike motion of fingers. It is fine, however, to use the thumb and forefinger together (which is a different motion) and traditional Navajos always used to hold a cigarette in this way. The sense of the whole taboo is to avoid behaving like an animal — any animal — because the behavior isn't proper and may offend the animal being mimicked, in which case the power of that animal will hurt you in some way or at least attract unwelcome attention from that animal.

A. Don't watch snakes having intercourse.
B. You'll go blind.

Like the dog going to the bathroom, one should avoid watching private actions of any kind and hopefully others will have the same consideration. On a more serious level when

90

a Navajo sees two snakes entwined — presumably in coitus — he should kill them at once, especially if he has a pregnant wife. This overrides the general taboo of leaving snakes alone and not killing them. Presumably it is the twining that causes the problem (related to tying knots, braiding etc.), but the fear of twined serpents seems more elemental and deepseated than that.

A. Don't step on a snake.

B. Your legs will swell up — get crooked.

A. Don't draw in the sand with your fingers.

B. Snakes will come to it.

Snakes, crawling through the sand, have no choice but to leave marks of their passing. The sense here, besides the avoidance of animal mimicry already mentioned, also seems to involve the power of drawn — and now written — symbols. This is apparently an extension of the power of the spoken word. Drawing in the sand also involves an activity much like sandpainting which is sacred in nature and must be limited to ceremonial contexts and undertaken by trained practitioners. There are a number of similar prohibitions, including the taboo of drawing or writing on one's person. Though many young Navajos ignore this, tatoos are the same class of activity and are prohibited.

A. Don't talk about snakes.

B. They will come around.

A. Don't laugh at a snake.

B. It will bite you.

A. Don't make faces at a snake.

B. It will bite you some day.

Slide your feet to break a snake's trail

A. Don't spit at a snake.
B. It will get after you.

A. Don't watch a snake crawl out of its skin.
B. You'll get sick or jump out of your skin.

A. Don't shoot an arrow at a snake.
B. It will go crooked — hit something else — be spoiled.

A. Don't run over a snake in your car.
B. You'll have a bad life.

A. Don't break snake eggs.
B. The snakes will get you.

This is a curious taboo only because rattlesnakes and most
snakes of the Southwest are viviparous — give live birth —
and I've never seen a snake egg.

*A. Don't wear anything made out of snakeskin, especial-
ly boots or shoes.*
B. You will get crippled.

A. Don't touch a snake.
B. It has nothing and it will make you have nothing.

I like this taboo because of its gentle way of making a state-
ment. Man should have consideration for the animal world
— simply because he has so much more than the animals, if
for no other reason. Snakes have no hands or feet, labor across
the burning sand, and have no worldly goods. They are lowest
of the low and molesting them suggests to the Supernaturals
that the person doing so is not appreciative of his position and
his own gifts.

A. Don't call a person a snake.
B. You'll be bitten by one.

A. Don't urinate on roads that cross each other.
B. That is the same as a snake trail.

BEARS

Some of the taboos associated with bears are probably a result of their rather human appearance when they stand upright. Bears are also the principle figures in a major Navajo ceremony, the Mountain Way. Some people claim that the Navajos considered bears to be reincarnated ancestors, but I have never known a Navajo who believed this.

The bear taboos all share a common motif, that if a human being mimics a wild animal he will become like that animal. In the case of bears the taboo is more potent because of the humanlike resemblance and because bears are one of the were-animals associated with witchcraft. There are other bear taboos scattered through the categories.

A. Don't step on a bear's waste.
B. It will bother you — you'll act like a bear.

A. Don't make fun of a bear.
B. It will make you sick.

A. Don't step on rocks turned over by a bear.
B. Bears will chase you.

A. Don't walk over a bear track.
B. You'll get hairy — can't get off — act crazy.

A. Don't step on a bear track.
B. You'll turn into a skinwalker.

Navajos have a number of bear taboos

A. Don't put your shoes on the wrong feet.
B. Bears do that — will get after you.

This is a reference to the story of the Night Animals and the Day Animals playing a shoe (moccasin) game to see if it would remain day or night permanently. Of course the game ended in a tie, thank goodness. But the weary bear, in a hurry to get his moccasins on, put them on the wrong feet. The bear's toes seem to turn out rather than inward, like a person's.

A. Don't say "Shush" (bear) in the mountains.
B. Bears will come to you.

A. Don't laugh at bears.
B. They will get after you.

DOMESTIC ANIMALS

Even in the last decade of the Twentieth Century Navajos have strong feelings about the value of horses, cattle and sheep, once the backbone of Navajo economy and the mark of personal wealth and status. Huge numbers of unbroken horses roam the reservation, eating up valuable grass that would support cows or sheep, but no Navajo takes kindly to the idea that these "worthless" animals should be disposed of. They, like the wild mustang in other parts of the West, symbolize the spirit of the Old Days. The Navajo were known as excellent horsemen and their horsemanship is mentioned in the works of many early explorers and chroniclers. A man's status was counted as much by the number of horses he owned as any single thing or accomplishment.

While most traditional Navajos are not particularly tenderhearted toward animals, and often seem to be somewhat cruel to pets, livestock has both intrinsic and extrinsic value and is cared for accordingly.

A. Don't say bad things about your livestock.
B. Something bad will happen to them.

A. Don't kill a sheep or goat that is unusual, has three horns or both sexes.
B. They are good luck — you'll lose your flock.

99

Never throw rocks at your sheep

A. Don't count your sheep too much.
B. Your flock will get smaller.

A. Don't clap at sheep.
B. Things will happen to them — you'll have a small herd.

A. Don't put a sheep's head on the ground upright.
B. It will go away — you'll lose your herd.

A. Don't play with a ball when you are herding sheep.
B. The lambs will be born deformed.

A. Don't throw things at the sheep.
B. They will disappear.

A. Don't ride on a sheep's back.
B. As punishment you'll be hurt bad.

A. Don't waste any part of the animal after butchering.
B. Your flock will be less.

A. Don't let a nanny goat have sex with a ram.
B. You'll lose their babies — they'll be sterile.

A. Don't castrate a ram, billygoat, stallion or other breeding animal when they are older.
B. They will go wild — crazy.

A. Don't burn livestock manure.
B. You are burning the animals too.

Navajos don't seem to mind selling the compacted manure from old sheep pens to Hopis who burn it to fire their pottery.

A. Don't kill too many sheep at the same time.
B. The herd won't like it — will disappear — run away.

Earmarking a horse will make it stupid

A. Don't burn wool.

B. Your sheep will be poor — something will happen to them.

A. Don't play with the horn of a goat.

B. One will bother you — bad luck for the herd.

A. Don't twist goats' tails.

B. They might come off — bad luck.

A. Don't go to sleep while you are herding sheep.

B. A crow might take your eyes out.

Another taboo which refers to a mythological tale. Crow lost his eyes as a result of violating the taboo against looking over the brush corral at a Fire Dance.[12] Crows will take advantage of human carelessness and sloth to steal a new pair of eyes. Stay alert when you have a responsibility to discharge.

A. Don't say "I wish I had some meat" when you have the hiccups.

B. Your livestock won't grow.

A. Don't cut the tips of a horse's ears off — earmark.

B. He will be stupid — hard to manage.

A. Don't burn horsehair.

B. You'll lose your horses.

A. Don't ride a pregnant animal or make it work hard.

B. It will lose the baby and never give birth again.

A. Don't watch a horse or other animal give birth.

B. You'll go blind.

A. Don't cut a horse's tail.

B. It will fall off a cliff.

Never cut off a horse's tail

A. Don't leave deer blood where sheep can walk on it.
B. All the wool will fall out.

A. Don't let your sheep or yourself walk on a deerskin.
B. They will go crazy — run away.

A couple of the many taboos which separate wild and domestic animals, as though traditional Navajos were a little ashamed of the fact that sheep supplanted deer as the staple of their diet and economy. Many of the early references to Navajos in the Spanish documents, for example, mention their trading of buckskins and dried venison to the Pueblos and Spanish for corn, peaches and other staples.

A. Don't spit on anyone.
B. You'll owe him livestock — a white stallion.

A. Don't eat livestock killed by a coyote or other wildanimals.
B. You'll go crazy — act wild.

A. Don't put a rug over the head of a horse.
B. He'll go blind.

MAN'S BEST FRIEND

The dog was the first domestic animal known to the Navajo people, though the first reciprocal relationship between man and dog is lost in the ancient past. As important as the dog has been to man throughout history — watchdog, beast of burden, source of hair for weaving material, occasional source of food, companion — Navajos seem to have an unusually ambivalent feeling about dogs. They are never completely comfortable with their pets, keeping them outdoors and seldom being especially affectionate with them. The dog, probably as an extension of Coyote/Wolf, is believed to have some magical powers, but uses them mostly for ill.

Coyote, as mentioned, is a very important figure in Navajo mythology and I am surprised there are not more taboos which mention him. It is safe to say that Dog inherits some of Coyote's characteristics in Navajo thinking and therefore dog and coyote are sometimes interchangeable.

Interestingly, in the Coyote tales the Coyote is usually the buffoon, the butt of the joke, the antisocial goof-off and screw-up — until he meets Dog. In the body of Coyote/Dog tales (most of which are dirty jokes), Dog becomes the victim and Coyote the clever keeper of tradition. In many of the stories where Coyote tricks Dog it is clear that Coyote represents traditional

Navajos and Dog the gullible, unsuspecting, rather stupid Anglo "tourist". Why not?

It seems logical to collect the dog taboos together, not because there are a such a great number of them, but because many of them are puzzling. The taboos against watching dogs go to the bathroom, or mate, specifically refer to not staring, especially at any private act, and "dog" is something of a euphemism for another person, though the taboo is considered to be literally true as well.

All the same, the penalty is a bit extreme and probably the real meaning of these taboos is as a euphemism for any unhealthy act of voyeurism. It is interesting that in these taboos, and others elsewhere in the list, domestic animals are not valued on any sort of emotional level and are actually feared, if anything.

A. Don't buy dog or cat for a pet.
B. You'll get poor.

Over the years I have discovered that I have, consciously or unconsciously, picked up a lot of Navajo attitudes and behaviors, including observing many of the taboos. This is one I have been particularly aware of. The world is full of unwanted animals in the first place, and most of us have better things to do with our money than buy funny looking dogs that cost hundreds of dollars just to satisfy some aspect of our vanity. With patience a person can usually come up with almost any breed of dog he desires without paying a lot of money for it. And who needs the silly paperwork anyway? There is also an obvious difference between sharing your house, food and companionship with an animal and "owning" that same

109

creature, with all the implications of ownership. Navajos are perhaps not especially sensitive to this last issue, since they prefer to keep pets at a distance, but the taboo makes good sense, all the same. I guess I'm just a country boy at heart.

A. *Don't open the eyes of newborn kittens or puppies.*
B. *You'll go blind.*

A. *Don't kill dogs.*
B. *They belong to spirits — you'll be paralyzed.*

The only breed of dog I find specifically mentioned in myths and historical tales is the Chihuahua, which was prized as a watchdog and seems to have claimed special affection from the Spirits.

A. *Don't brand a dog as a joke.*
B. *You'll lose your livestock.*

A. *Don't choke a kitten.*
B. *You'll have throat trouble.*

A. *Don't watch dogs have intercourse.*
B. *You'll go blind.*

A. *Don't watch a dog go to the bathroom.*
B. *You'll go crazy.*

A. *Don't give food from a ceremony to the dogs.*
B. *It will spoil the ceremony.*

A. *Don't let a dog bite the Medicine man.*
B. *The sing won't work.*

A. *Don't talk to dogs - other animals.*
B. *They might talk back which means you will die.*

It's not a good idea to talk to your dog

A. Don't play too much with dogs (girls).
B. They will try to mate with you.

A. Don't let dogs follow you around (girls).
B. They may get fresh with you.

A. Don't let a dog eat in front of you when you butcher.
B. You'll lose the meat.

THE POWER OF THE WORD

We have already seen a number of taboos involving animals that properly belong in this section which deals with the power, the literal magic, of language. There are numerous prohibitions against saying the names of certain animals or speaking to them as if they were human. The power of the spoken (and written) word is one of the more universal areas of human belief, though the so-called sophisticated peoples of the world have, perhaps, perverted this power in some ways. Probably the incredible advances in mass communications have been largely responsible for the change in attitude toward the power of the word, but the fact is that Anglo-Americans have lost their appreciation of the magic of language.

One of the best scenes in N. Scott Momaday's prize-winning novel *House Made of Dawn* has an Indian character give a fine oration on the subject. According to the Reverend Big Bluff Tosamah, we Anglos are in the process of talking ourselves out of existence. He is not altogether correct in asserting that the White Man fails to appreciate the power of language, as the work of any of our poets will quickly prove. The great e. e. cummings created a world that was mud-luscious and puddle-wonderful and that's proof enough for me. At any rate we HAVE destroyed the value of many of our words through the abuses of advertising, through neglect, through misuse and overuse.

Modern writers have had to go beyond the word itself for their effects, which may account for the interest currently in

113

It is dangerous to make fun of old people

the cinema as a literary form. The traditional Indian, however, has maintained respect for the power of the word when he has been lucky enough to preserve his native language, as the Navajos have. Speech, to a traditional Navajo, is not a magic to be taken lightly, and the individual has to take responsibility for what comes out of his mouth.

In the greater context, recall that Adam's first act in the Garden was to name the animals, and having named them, to be given power over them. The word is equal to the thing. In many ages and many societies a person's name has been considered a powerful thing, and only a close friend may know one's true name.

Many cultures have such beliefs or vestigial remains of such beliefs. The childhood rite of bestowing nicknames undoubtedly stems from this set of beliefs. In some fraternities the individual gets a special name or nickname. Catholics, for another instance, name children after the patron saint of their birth date. One modern Christian religion has a naming ritual as part of the wedding ceremony. In secret the man and woman are given new names. The husband knows the wife's secret name and must use it to call her into the highest kingdom of heaven. She is not told his special name.

We would all get along better if we could regain our respect for the power of the word, and if a man's word again became a matter of honor. Certainly one of modern man's most discussed dilemmas is his inability to communicate with his fellow man. The following taboos reflect a respect for the power of words.

A. *Don't say "chindi" (evil spirit).*
B. *One will come to you and do you harm.*

We have seen this taboo several times before. Calling the name of a snake, bear or other dangerous creature will also call its unwanted attention to the speaker. The overlying principle here has already been discussed. The name of a thing — especially a person, a supernatural or a dangerous animal — had great power in and of itself. The general rule is, watch what you say and don't speak carelessly at any time.

A. Don't use the name of a dead person.
B. The ghost will come visit you — bring you harm.

A. Don't talk about someone you don't actually know.
B. They might be dead and you'll call them.

The tremendous avoidance of the dead and their belongings is dealt with elsewhere. The significance here is, once again, that a person's name has great power, even after death.

A. Don't talk about killing yourself.
B. Someone else in your family will die in your place.

A. Don't thank people who help with a funeral.
B. They will be the next to die.

As a side issue, Navajos, before extensive Anglo contact and influence, used "please" and "thank you" sparingly and only when meant sincerely, not as table talk and empty formulaic behavior. In Navajo, the word "please" is considered to be begging and has a whiny sound to it. In this case the reason for withholding thanks is more important in that it might cause unwanted attention from the evil spirits.

A. Don't pretend to pray or cry for no reason.
B. Someone in your family will die — you are wishing for that.

Navajos avoid mean or vulgar talk

A. Don't laugh or make jokes at old people.
B. Some day you'll be worse than them.

A. Don't lie about yourself.
B. Bad things will come true.

A. Don't say your own name too much.
B. Your ears will dry up.

A. Don't use your own name.
B. You'll wear it out — have bad luck — your ears will fall off.

A. Don't make up names for yourself.
B. You'll get a bad name.

A. Don't tell your age.
B. You'll grow old faster.

A. Don't brag about your valuable things.
B. You'll lose them.

A. Don't criticize any poor family.
B. You'll get worse than them.

A. Don't tell a person to go to hell.
B. It might happen.

A. Don't keep secrets from your grandmother.
B. You'll get old before your time.

A. Don't talk about your illness.
B. You'll have a worse one.

A. Don't make plans at night for the next day.
B. They won't come true.

A. Don't say nasty things to your relatives — sisters.
B. You'll go crazy — jump into the fire.

Written symbols, like words, have power to cause harm

A. Don't tell lies about a girl (boys bragging about sexual affairs).

B. She might be your sister and you'll go crazy.

These two are examples of the extension of the incest taboo. The word is considered equivalent to the deed. The second one refers to the danger of carelessness in relationships. The girl may be, unbeknownst to the speaker, a clan sister or relative.

PERSONAL BEHAVIOR

This category especially illustrates the fact that these taboos were originally collected from and by young people and many of them are obviously aimed at behavior control. All the same, there is an emphasis on preserving individual privacy and respect for the rights of other people — in modern parlance, respecting their "space". There is also, here and elsewhere, a respect for thrift, cautious behavior, enterprise, and common sense.

A. Don't laugh when someone pollutes the air.
B. You'll get wrinkles right away.

A. Don't wash your face with really hot water.
B. You'll get old faster.

A. Don't pull out white hairs.
B. You'll get more.

A. Don't go to bed after washing your hair without brushing it.
B. You'll die of thirst some day.

A. Don't count your blackheads.
B. They get worse.

A. Don't chew your fingernails.
B. They won't grow back — you'll go broke.

A. Don't cry during a funeral.
B. You'll get bags under your eyes.

A. Don't rub tree bark on your body.
B. It will make you hairy.

A. Don't put salt on your hair or eat too much salt.
B. Your hair will turn white.

A. Don't cut your hair.
B. You won't be able to think well — have a short life.

A. Don't look at a tooth that has fallen out.
B. The others will fall out too.

A. Don't put your shoes on the wrong feet.
B. You'll go crazy — run away.

This is a disguised bear taboo. In the story of the first Shoe Game, which gave the world night and day, Bear, in his great haste, put his moccasins on the wrong feet. Bear tracks seem to toe out, rather than in as human feet do. Acting like a bear always causes wild and crazy behavior.

A. Don't try to cut limbs off a tree while it is still standing.
B. You'll chop yourself.

A. Don't be lazy when you are young (boys).
B. You'll act like a woman.

A. Don't walk around in your long-johns at night.
B. You'll frighten your children - look like a ghost.

A. Don't hate persons of the opposite sex — especially any ugly one.
B. You might end up marrying them.

Literally, you will be punished in life by having to endure all the things you have no patience with or understanding for. There are variations of this taboo which prohibit laughing at unfortunate people, gossiping about them, or similar activities.

On a literal level this taboo refers back to the days when families often arranged marriages for their children, who had no choice in the matter.

Years ago I noticed that Navajos were rather less impressed with superficial things like good looks and clothes in their choice of mates anyway.

A. Don't wear your blanket with the stripes crossways.
B. You'll go crazy.

A. Don't make fingers (like obscene gestures).
B. You'll cripple your hand.

A. Don't stare at anyone for a long time.
B. You'll go blind.

A. Don't lend your shirt to anyone.
B. He will get all of your good luck.

A. Don't follow in someone's footprints.
B. You'll get crippled.

A. Don't put your fingers on top of each other — cross your fingers.
B. You'll act like a baby.

A. Don't play around an ash dump.
B. You'll get hunchbacked.

A. Don't smoke unless you have caught a female coyote on foot.
B. It will cause you harm — stunt your growth.

This is a classic Navajo euphemism. The reference to catching

Lazy boys turn effeminate

a female coyote really means to have come of age — literally, to have had sexual relations. The sense of it is that you should be an adult to smoke. The less obvious meaning is that if you wait to do things like smoking until you have a little wisdom and experience, you probably won't do them at all. Though tobacco came from the Indians originally, they used it only in a ceremonial context and not recreationally. The use of pipes, ceremonial cigarettes and other tobacco is still central to most Native American religious observance.

A. Don't break sticks.
B. You'll have bad luck.

This doesn't refer to breaking up kindling while building a fire, for example. It is meant to be a reference to the fact that implements used in a funeral are broken and left at the gravesite. To idly sit about and snap sticks would seem to be imitating funeral behavior which might confuse any evil spirits lurking about and draw their attention.

A. Don't have three people comb each other's hair at the same time.
B. They'll get stuck.

A. Don't take a doll apart.
B. It will make you sick — crippled — it might affect your children.

This is both a reference to sympathetic magic — the doll representing a child — and witchcraft as mentioned under "Sleep."

A. Don't store jewelry like beads in a heap — hang them up.
B. You'll lose them — they'll be unhappy and cramped.

125

A. Don't undo a string of beads.

B. They'll disappear.

A. Don't store turquoise beads in a plastic bag or airtight container.

B. They'll die — won't be able to breathe — will turn no good.

Turquoise seems to have a soul of its own. It is a very soft material which is easily affected by body oils, soap, heat and many other things. Beads stored in plastic DO seem to lose their life — zat — and become chalky and dull. Observing this phenomenon is likely to reinforce the idea that turquoise is a living thing. At any rate, Turquoise, like any valuable thing, is entitled to respect and proper care. In many homes beads are hung on nails high up on the wall (out of reach of children and idle curiosity) and are then covered with some cloth or hanging decoration. To be really safe, they are pawned and redeemed when needed for a ceremony or festive occasion.

A. Don't leave an arrowhead lying on the ground.

B. You'll lose the good luck they bring.

A. Don't pop a paper bag.

B. Your parents will go broke — pop your tonsils — get a goiter.

A. Don't turn pages backwards.

B. You'll go blind.

A. Don't draw the opposite sex (nasty drawings).

B. You won't be attractive.

A. Don't wish for a wife if you don't have one.

B. You'll never get one.

A. Don't talk nasty to anyone.

B. You'll jump in the fire.

A. Don't tell lies about a girl (boys bragging about sexual affairs).

B. They might be your sister (clan sister or relative).

A. Don't watch men going into a sweat bath.

B. You'll go crazy — blind.

A. Don't make fun of female clothing or sex organs.

B. Bad luck — that's where you came from.

A. Don't burn blood from a nosebleed.

B. You'll have headaches — your head will split.

Scattered through this list are a great number of taboos involving fire and ashes. Obviously fire is a wonderful tool and shouldn't be abused. Navajos, using wood stoves and open fires rather than electric ranges, water heaters and central furnaces, are more aware of flames and the power of fire for both good and evil. One reason to state this particular taboo is that blood, whatever its origin, must be disposed of properly. If left lying about (like hair, spit, nail parings) it can be used by a witch. Burning is a good way to get rid of any of this material. Nosebleeds are a special case, as noted in the taboo involving porcupines.

Notice also the large number of things that must not be burned — insects, hair, parts of wild animals, blood and so on. Fire seems to have an almost spiritual force, as though it were sentient somehow, a living thing, and objects and materials given to the fire are seen as "food." We commonly refer to "feeding" a fire, after all. Feeding it the wrong things would seem to encourage it to get out of control perhaps.

SLEEP

In many cultures the soul of a sleeping person is believed to leave the body, as in dreams, and wander about on its own. At this time the connection between soul and body is considered to be so weak — and the sleeping person so vulnerable, that stepping over the sleeping body is believed to cause great injury or even death, because the wandering soul gets cut off and cannot come back to the body. A sleeping person seems both helpless and vulnerable in any culture, and the activities of the soul during sleep as understood through dreams, is significant in almost all cultures.

Perhaps nearly as significant is the idea that a sleeping person is not attending to other important activities. One who sleeps too much will not get ahead in the world. A lot of sleeping is a sign of sloth, laziness, poor character and other negative characteristics. Elsewhere we have encountered taboos against sleeping during an eclipse, during a ceremony, during a lightning storm — all dangerous situations.

A. Don't sleep with your head pointing to the North.
B. You might die — north is the direction of evil — dead people lie that way.

A. Don't sleep with your head toward the head end of a sheepskin.
B. It will run off with you during the night.

This is the sort of taboo that's fun to laugh at because it

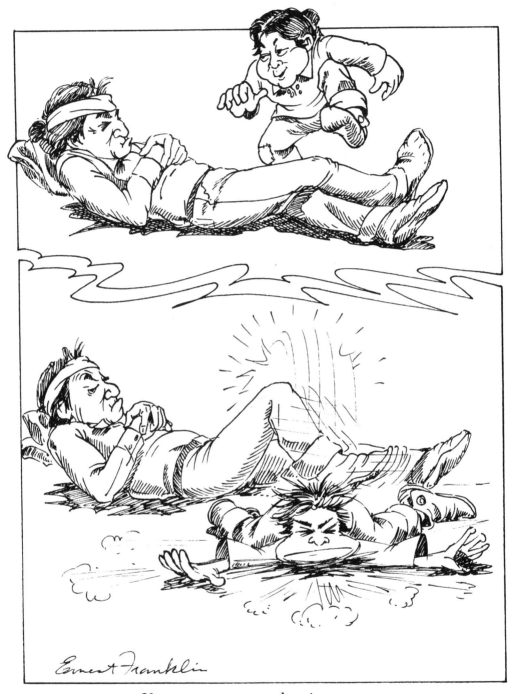

Never step over a sleeping person

sounds so strange to an Anglo and doesn't seem to make sense. Part of the reason is that, like many things to do with witches, it is stated in the form of a euphemism. Few Navajos would literally believe the sheepskin would carry the unwary sleeper away. Keep in mind that witches are not born that way. They are ordinary people who decide, of their own volition, that they are not content with the lot fate, the gods or their own laziness has cast them in. They want more goods, more power, more revenge, more money or whatever and elect to get these things through the practice of evil.

One of the common forms of witchcraft involves the were-animal (wolf, owl, bear or other creature) which the person turns into after donning an animal skin. When a person carelessly mimics this behavior, even innocently, he is betraying a bent personality, at the very least. At worst, his true nature will come out while he is in the weak sleep state, and he will be possessed.

All witching behaviors are not codified as taboos. There is no need to prohibit cannibalism, mutilation of corpses, necrophilia or other really aberrant behavior. The taboos are gentle reminders to avoid suspicious actions that might be practiced purely by accident.

Elsewhere you will find taboos against rings on forefingers, inside-out clothing, loose hair and other things that might be done out of ignorance.

A. Don't sleep with a doll.
B. It might choke you.

Navajos have a tendency to see dolls, mannequins and dummies as vaguely evil. Without raising issues of "voodoo",

131

Don't sleep with your head toward the head end of a sheepskin

witches use dolls sometimes to practice their evil. Best not to push one's luck.

A. Don't sleep too much or too late in the day.
B. You'll get old soon — have spots on your face.

A. Don't sleep at sunset.
B. You'll be sick often.

A. Don't leave your shoes under your pillow when you sleep.
B. You'll go deaf — have bad dreams.

A. Don't sleep with a cat or dog.
B. You'll have stomach trouble — get a bad smell inside of you.

A. Don't sleep with a rug under your head.
B. You won't sleep well — you'll have nightmares.

A. Don't use a rock for a pillow.
B. It will cause bad dreams — deform your head.

A. Don't put your arms on your chest when you sleep.
B. You won't wake up — you'll talk in your sleep.

A. Don't sleep with your socks on.
B. You won't get any rest.

A. Don't sleep with your hat on.
B. It will grow onto your head.

A. Don't walk over someone's leg while they are sleeping.
B. You'll get a leg ache.

A. Don't go to bed early in the evening.
B. The poverty people will come around.

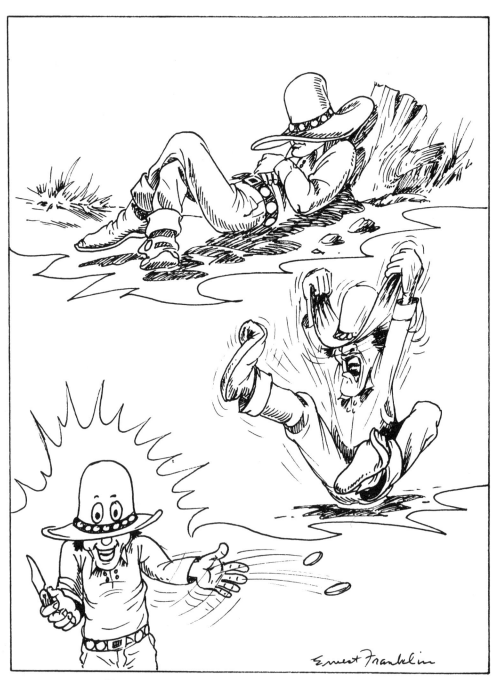

Sleeping in your hat may have side affects

A. Don't sleep past sunup.
B. All the good things will pass you by.

PREGNANCY

The large number of taboos concerning pregnancy and babies is typical of many cultures. Many of these undoubtedly date from the days, not so long ago, when infant mortality was extremely high, and only a couple of children of a large family were likely to reach maturity. Others predate knowledge of medicine and the germ theory of disease. Certainly the great concern for children is a factor of love as well as a necessary condition for the preservation of the race. Many of the beliefs about prenatal influences on the appearance and disposition of babies are still widely held in rural America, as well as other parts of the world.

In a way it is interesting that Navajos actually have a limited number of taboos in this category, all things considered. Most of the taboos seem to lump in a few classes: don't tie, weave, braid or plug things; avoid most animals, especially dead ones or those considered "evil" or dangerous anyway; and avoid strange or violent activity. Missing are logical taboos involving such things as diet; though excessive fat and sugar are to be avoided, almost nothing else is prohibited.

And traditional Navajos did not curtail or modify sexual

activity — some even say that the more sex during gestation the more the baby would look like the father, an interesting notion. Pregnancy taboos are among the most universal, found everywhere in the world.

A. Don't tie knots when you are pregnant.
B. You'll have a hard time having the baby.

A. Don't put bowls together when you are pregnant.
B. You'll have trouble having the baby.

A. Don't stand in a doorway while pregnant.
B. The baby won't come out.

A. Don't stand in the doorway when a pregnant women is present.
B. She will have trouble having the baby.

There are quite a number of related taboos. Anything, any activity, which seems to bind something up (like a man sewing on a saddle, below), to nail something shut to secure it, or to plug an opening is seen as improper activity for a pregnant woman — and by extension, her husband and perhaps other members of the family, at least while she is present. The most interesting example of the application of this taboo came up some years ago when I was giving talks for the Navajo Labor Department.

Various topics were presented to employees of companies doing business on the Reservation. The idea was to head off some recurrent problems before the damage was already done. Most of the presentations were given by Navajos, but they liked to have me talk about witchcraft and some related topics because it looks bad if a Navajo seems to know too much about

Be careful how you behave while pregnant

such things.

The situation was described where a Navajo man was fired from a job because he refused to take part in a first aid class which involved practicing CPR techniques on a dummy. The foreman telling the story challenged me to explain such foolish "insubordinate" behavior. In the first place, for many Navajos there would be extreme distaste — perhaps even very real fear — to put his mouth in the same place as many strangers, as in the case of going mouth to mouth with the dummy. But if the man's wife was pregnant the situation would be impossible, since blowing into the mannequin's mouth would either affect the unborn child, or significantly complicate the subsequent birth. Unfortunately, the man was embarrassed to explain such a personal taboo for fear of ridicule.

A. Don't wear two hats at the same time.
B. You'll have twins — two wives.

A. Don't try to count the stars.
B. You'll have too many children.

A. Don't make a circle around yourself.
B. You'll have a round baby.

A. Don't swallow gum while you are pregnant.
B. The baby will have a dark spot on it — birthmark.

A. Don't kill any animal while your wife is pregnant.
B. The baby will be born funny.

A. Don't kill birds while your wife is pregnant.
B. The baby will look like a bird.

A. Don't sew on a saddle while your wife is pregnant.
B.It will ruin the baby's mouth.

140

Two hats is a sure way to end up with twins

A. Don't make a slingshot while you are pregnant.
B. The baby will be crippled.

A. Don't look at any strange creatures while your wife is pregnant.
B. The baby will be born strange.

A. Don't go to ceremonies while pregnant.
B. It will have a bad effect on the baby.

A. Don't peel potatoes or apples when you are pregnant.
B. The baby will have a flat face.

A. Don't hit a sheep's legs while your wife is pregnant.
B. The baby will be crippled.

A. Don't yell at a pregnant woman.
B. The baby will be deaf.

A. Don't eat a lot of sweet stuff when you are pregnant.
B. The baby won't be strong.

A. Don't sleep too much when you are about to have a baby.
B. The baby will mark you in some way.

A. Don't look at a dead person while you are pregnant or dead animals.
B. Bad luck for the baby — it will be sickly.

A. Don't jump around if you are pregnant.
B. It will induce labor.

A. Don't eat too much fat stuff while pregnant.
B. The baby will have trouble coming out.

A. Don't kill a frog while your wife is pregnant.
B. The baby will walk or jump like a frog.

A. Don't look at a wild cat or other wild animals while pregnant.

B. The baby will look like that — be wild.

A. Don't cut gloves off at the knuckles.

B. Baby will have short, round fingers.

A. Don't put on a Yei mask while your wife is pregnant.

B. The baby will have a big head — look strange.

A. Don't carry small animals when you are pregnant.

B. The baby will look like that animal.

A. Don't cross your fingers.

B. It shows your mother is going to have a baby — or your father's ex-wife is pregnant.

A. Don't eat Navajo onion.

B. You'll have lots of kids.

A. Don't watch an accident while your wife is pregnant.

B. It will affect the baby.

A. Don't hit your wife while she is pregnant.

B. She'll lose the baby.

A. Don't tease your wife about pregnancy.

B. What you say will come true.

BABIES

While a child is in infancy it is considered to still be in a formative stage, physically as well as mentally, especially for the first few days or weeks — an extension of gestation. Traditionally, babies were not named right away and often naming was put off for a year or even more. An infant was not really considered a human being yet, and in the old days was so likely to die that wasting a name on it was careless, especially considering the taboos relating to names.

Newborns were simply referred to as "baby" and later "child" with some descriptive term appended"red child" or the like. There was a stock of baby names including the famous "Laughing Boy."[13] The baby name would gradually be discarded after the real naming, though not immediately since the "real" name was kept secret from all but a few family members. Sometimes children were designated by number like "first son", or relationships like "elder brother."

At any rate, babies were (and are) considered especially vulnerable to all of life's many dangers and were traditionally raised both protectively and indulgently.[14] They were often kept bound in a cradle board for the first two years of life which is VERY protective.

145

A. Don't make an infant laugh while it is still tiny.

B. It's dangerous — will affect it later — it won't laugh when it grows up.

This is one of my favorite taboos since it relates to a Navajo belief that I find especially significant and delightful. As discussed above, newborns were not really considered to be human beings, and idea found in many cultures where life is difficult. But what marks the turning point? First birthday? Reaching three feet tall? Learning to walk? The first spoken word or intelligent utterance might be a nice choice. In many cultures such signs were considered significant. But for Navajos the turning point was the first spontaneous laugh. Perhaps having a sense of humor IS what makes us human beings, after all. It is certainly a wonderful choice.

As soon as the baby laughed the grandmother or some other significant elder would be called in and a naming ceremony held, a very significant rite of passage. "Real" names were often chosen from a stock — or followed a certain formula. No child, however, would be named for a grandparent or any deceased person.

A. Don't get after babies or cuss at them.

B. They will be worse.

A. Don't tease babies or hurt them.

B. They will think bad about you and you will be like that.

A. Don't hold a mirror up to a baby.

B. The baby will go blind.

Mirrors and their strange magic have been discussed before.

The operational idea here is that a newborn, or infant is still somewhat unformed (which we talked about in connection with names) and is easily affected by things that will not harm an adult. Since mirrors always have the possibility of danger, exposing a child to their power holds special risks. Navajos, like many other Native American groups, are very indulgent parents and young children are disciplined gently or not at all. After a certain age the child is expected to behave properly. Most teaching is by example rather than explanation or exhortation.

A. Don't cut a baby's hair when it is small.
B. It won't think right when it gets older.

Actually a traditional Navajo might not believe in cutting hair at all. For one thing, the traditional hair style — worn by both men and women — was quite distinctive, a large bun at the back of the neck, and was another badge of Navajoness. The Bureau of Indian Affairs would give boy children a GI haircut as the first act of civilizing them and long hair for men is gradually coming back into vogue as a reassertion of identity. People also say that early hair cutting, besides making the child think "wrongly", would make it stupid, belligerent, willful, or have other bad effects.

A. Don't hit babies in the mouth.
B. They'll be stubborn — slow to talk.

A. Don't allow a cat near a new baby.
B. The cat will suffocate it.

Here is that fear of domestic animals again, though other cultures share this idea about cats, who like to curl up next to people's heads for some reason.

A. *Don't give babies things you really like.*
B. *The baby might die.*

This one has several points of significance. As mentioned above, infant mortality used to be very high so there was danger in giving them things of value. On the one hand such possessions might be considered by the supernaturals as bragging or showing off, and the child be punished — taken away. Ownership among Navajos is rather different than Anglos see it. If a child "owns" something, even a valuable heirloom like an old bow and arrow set, it is his to dispose of and the adults would likely not interfere if he sold it or punish him if he broke it. If the child shouldn't have had the item in the first place this taboo should have been in effect. If the baby died naturally, the item, perhaps valuable jewelry, would have to be buried with it since no one can keep things which belong to a dead person. Thus the wealth would be taken away from the family.

A. *Don't leave a baby's track on the ground.*
B. *A witch can use the track to hurt the baby.*

In the Hero Twins Tale the monsters are told about the existence of the two boys when they are first born and come around to kill them. Changing Woman, their mother, denies she has any babies but the monsters see the footprints in the dust. Changing Woman explains this away by saying she was so lonely she pretended to have children and made the tracks with her fingers.

As stated several times, children are considered to be somewhat unformed — not yet seasoned — and are thus very vulnerable. Even a track is personal enough to make an evil

149

Babies shouldn't cross their fingers

connection.

A. Don't tell little children giant stories.

B. They'll be stupid.

Most of the giant stories portray the giants (monsters of an earlier age) as very stupid and, as children are impressionable, they shouldn't hear these stories. Most of the giant stories I know are also bawdy and few of them have been collected and published with other Navajo folktales, primarily excepting those which are also Coyote stories.

A. Don't leave a baby alone at night.

B. Ghosts might shock him.

A. Don't take a baby outside at night without ashes.

B. Ghosts might harm it.

A. Don't let a baby suck its thumb.

B. The nail won't grow.

This is obviously a modern addition and the reason given is a lame one. Traditionally, a child kept in a cradleboard had his arms bound to his sides and couldn't put anything in his mouth. Infants got a lot of attention from mother and other family members and things were tied at eye level to distract his attention. His pacifiers were visual rather than physical.

A. Don't hold a baby upside down.

B. It will have a flat front.

A. Don't let a baby's head stay to one side in the cradle board.

B. It will have a wide head.

A. Don't change a baby girl's diaper (boys).

B. You might go blind.

Another extension of the incest taboo, discussed at length in the introduction. There are other taboos which deal with activities which are sex specific. Navajos, like other cultures, permitted boys and girls only activities considered appropriate to their sex. Changing diapers would be considered women's work in any case and male chauvinism is still pretty universal on the Reservation.

A. Don't let a baby cross it's fingers.
B. Its mother will have another one right away.

Finger crossing comes up several times as an apparently sexual gesture but I don't understand its further significance.

AROUND THE HOGAN

Much is made of the fact that most Native American houses were circular in design rather than square or rectangular. Obviously the available building materials had a lot to do with the shape of the structure. From rather early times the fabulous stone masons of the Southwest built houses with corners. Structurally, round is the ONLY way to put together a tepee or lodge. The original Navajo home, the Hogan, was like a permanent tepee with a porch over the door. It also somewhat resembled a dirt igloo. Since most of the trees in the Southwest are rather short, the possible designs are limited.

I have read and heard learned discussions about why hogans "always" have six walls. Or "always" has eight sides, if that is the case. I asked several oldtime Navajos for their opinion on the subject and they replied, "It depends on how long the logs are, or how big you want to make it." Makes sense to me. At any rate, most hogans are small, poorly ventilated, and rather hard to heat in really cold weather because of the smoke hole in the roof.

On the other hand they are solid, tend to be cool in hot weather, turn their backs to sandstorms and last almost forever (unless someone happens to die in them, when they must be destroyed or abandoned). Some of the taboos relating to the house are extensions of other matters, but many come from the pressures of a number of people living in cramped quarters

Rude visitors often have bad luck

with little or no privacy. The privacy taboos are virtually a category of their own.

A. Don't face your house any direction but East, toward the sunrise.

B. Evil will come in - good luck won't find the door.

A. Don't go immediately up to the door when you approach a house.

B. You might be bringing evil spirits with you - bad things that have followed you.

This is rural etiquette in many places. Immediately stepping out of your car (down from the wagon, in the old days) is asking for a dog attack, if nothing else. Rural folk don't get a lot of visitors and sometimes need a minute to get properly dressed, put objects away, clean up the house or whatever.

At least to call off the dogs and invite a person in. In earlier times the mountain men considered it good behavior to hail a campfire before approaching.

A. Don't go through a window unless you go back the same way.

B. You won't grow.

There are ceremonies where the patient is passed through hoops in order to symbolically change his form, as Coyote did in mythological times. Passing through a window would mimic this behavior.

A. Don't go to the right of the stove when you visit someone.

B. You will cause yourself or them harm.

A. Don't climb through the smokehole of the hogan.

B. Bad luck - that is the entrance for good and bad spirits.

A. Don't run around the stove.

B. Your hogan will burn up.

A. Don't throw your hat around in the house.

B. You'll go crazy.

This is one of several hat taboos which shows the connection between the head covering and the head itself. In earlier times headwear was often ceremonial in nature — associated with war (like the feather bonnets) or other special activities. The traditional Navajo headgear was a leather beanie affair which often had fetishes, turquoise, arrowheads and other things attached, along with a few feathers. Lion skin caps were, and still are worn at certain times. Almost no Navajo man will go anywhere without his cowboy hat on, and it is not considered particularly good form to bother taking it off at the table while eating, while riding in the pickup, or anywhere else, except bed (where it is tabooed).

A. Don't leave the door closed all the time during the day.

B. You'll shut out good things.

A. Don't leave your house messy or dirty.

B. That will invite the poverty people.

A. Don't climb on top of the hogan.

B. You'll bring bad luck to your family.

A. Don't leave a bucket of ashes around the house.

B. You'll drive away good things - invite the poverty people.

Running around your hogan is just asking for trouble

A. Don't look at your mother-in-law or speak to her.
B. You'll go blind — have trouble.

The mother-in-law taboo is a well known one and is considered quite humorous by many Anglos but, until fairly recently, was taken very seriously by traditional Navajos. The older woman would even wear bells sewn to her clothing so the husbands wouldn't run into her inadvertently. Since Navajos were matrilocal, that is, lived at the wife's home, there might be several men in residence who had to avoid her at the same time. Much information on this subject is scattered about in the literature.

A. Don't look at a couple sleeping together.
B. You'll go blind.

A. Don't watch a person dress.
B. You'll go blind.

A. Don't look at a nude woman (boys).
B. You'll go blind.

A. Don't be nude in front of your sisters and relatives (boys).
B. You'll make them go blind.

FOOD AND COOKING

This category includes some of the most familiar taboos. Such proverbs as "A watched pot never boils," and "Too many cooks spoil the broth," are still commonly heard in rural America. The large number of taboos relating to food, household objects and food preparation is accounted for by the social nature of cooking and eating and the frequency with which both are done. All Navajo ceremonies involve the feeding of large numbers of guests and a great deal of socializing goes on at meal times. Navajos are also known for their hospitality and on at least one occasion I unknowingly ate the last food in the house, while the family watched me and assured me they had plenty.

The Navajos have also known extreme poverty and hunger in years of war or drought when the crops failed. The Enemy Way tells of the Warrior Twins sparing Hunger because one must know want to appreciate plenty.

A. Don't eat with your hat on.
B. You won't get full.

One of the first things visitors often notice in the Southwest is that etiquette about hat wearing doesn't seem to apply. In almost any restaurant the men, Anglo and Indian alike, will all be eating with their cowboy hats firmly on their heads.

One reason is undoubtedly the fact that hats, felt or straw, have gotten ridiculously expensive and they are easy to steal if left unattended in a cafe. For Navajos, though, this is a personal item of apparel which comes in contact that the head, a vulnerable part of the body. A person who wished you ill could put something bad in your hat which would affect you later. Most Navajo men are seldom seen without a hat on in any social occasion.

A. Don't damage things you have eaten from.
B. They do that when you die.

A. Don't eat from broken or cracked cooking utensils.
B. Only evil spirits do that — you'll be witched.

Keep in mind that all ghosts are evil spirits to a Navajo. There is not such thing as a "good" ghost. Whatever remains behind of a person who dies is automatically evil and wishes ill to those who are still living. In ancient times all personal objects and some household items were sent off with the deceased. To avoid another person using these things accidently they were broken and made unusable.

Once upon a time it was not uncommon to find saddles hung in trees in remote areas. This was a burial item and as such the saddle tree would often be broken so the saddle couldn't be used. By extension, broken objects should be disposed of so others won't suspect the family of violating a serious taboo.

And a visitor would refuse the use of a broken object for fear they had done just that. Finally, with the proudness of the poor, Navajos have always tried to keep their few possessions in good repair and avoid, by sloppiness and sloth,

160

attracting attention from the "hunger people."

A. Don't feed Navajo cake to a dog.
B. It won't taste good next time.

A. Don't eat your own Navajo cake (girls).
B. Your teeth will fall out.

A. Don't eat a Navajo cake all by yourself.
B. Your teeth will fall out.

Navajo cake is made with sweetened cornmeal and is usually only prepared on ceremonial occasions, like a girl's puberty ceremony. Since such a cake, baked in a pit in the ground, is very large, the idea here probably refers to a piece of cake brought back from some ceremony. The tooth reference is obvious, given the sweet nature of the food, but the real point is that one should never be greedy or selfish. There is also a general taboo against doing anything to excess.

At a large meal, I have seen the diners tear the last piece of fry bread into smaller and smaller and smaller pieces, but no one will take the last bite. Finally, there used to be a tradition that a bit of any food or beverage be thrown to the ground as a sort of generic offering to any spirits that might be in the vicinity. They would be angered if one were so stingy as to keep every bite. This is also a symbolic gesture to Mother Earth who provides all nourishment in the first place.

A. Don't stab a knife point first into meat or other food.
B. You'll have sharp pains inside.

A. Don't eat with a knife.
B. You'll have backaches — lose your livestock.

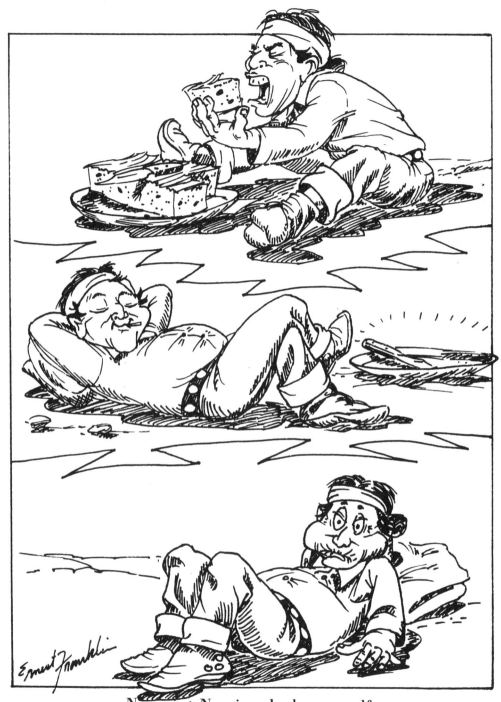

Never eat Navajo cake by yourself

Flint, the original material of knives, is very sacred in Navajo culture and even has a ceremony of its own, "Flintway." It was probably held in high regard, not just because of its obvious value in toolmaking, but because of the far northern origin of the Athabascan stock to which the Navajos belong.

Where flint was scarce it would naturally be highly prized. By extension the word for flint is also the word for knife — *besh* — and, when steel knives were introduced, became the word for steel. Beyond that, a valuable tool should only be used for the purpose it was intended, not treated casually or disrespectfully.

A. Don't leave meat joints together.
B. They'll run off (you'll lose them) — you'll have rheumatism.

This is another taboo whose underlying meaning is, don't show off, don't be lazy, don't be greedy. A serving of meat is properly the amount that belongs to a specific bone of the animal. To serve (or take) the whole carcass, or whole leg even, would be a violation of polite behavior. The immediate effect would be to have no success hunting, lose your stock, or have your own body punished by pain.

A. Don't eat from stacked dishes.
B. Someday you'll starve to death.

A. Don't put the cap back on any empty bottle.
B. You'll get a headache.

A. Don't put a bowl, Navajo basket, or bucket on your head.
B. You won't grow any more.

A. Don't eat without feeding something to the fire.
B. You'll never be rich.

A variation of the gesture mentioned above where the individual drops a morsel to the ground as an offering to the spirits or the earth. The tool of fire is so central to comfortable existence, and food preparation in particular, that a symbolic acknowledgement of this is important. It is not so much that the fire is seen to be sentient and therefor thankful, but that the individual never lose sight of the gifts he has received from the physical and spiritual worlds.

A. Don't cook ribs inside up.
B. You'll get divorced.

This may be a joking reference since, over a fire or bed of coals, the rack of ribs will be turned over and over during cooking and both sides will be cooked.

A. Don't eat from a pot that is still cooking.
B. You'll starve to death someday.

A. Don't eat the heel of a loaf of bread.
B. You'll have lots of children.

This is another taboo that I have found in many other cultures. Jewish men are not supposed to take the end of the loaf.

A. Don't eat, kick, or look at mushrooms.
B. You'll go blind.

A. Don't eat in front of a dog.
B. He'll get full and you'll stay hungry.

A. Don't eat things like the meat of bears or snakes.
B. You'll go wild — be crazy.

A. *Don't count things you are cooking (fry bread).*
B. *They will decrease.*

A. *Don't waste meat.*
B. *Your livestock will go away.*

A. *Don't shoot an animal you are going to eat — butcher it some other way.*
B. *The meat will spoil.*

A. *Don't eat any livestock killed by a snake.*
B. *It will poison you.*

A. *Don't eat on a rock.*
B. *You'll get heavy as a rock.*

A. *Don't drink pop when you are drunk.*
B. *Won't mix — worse headache — get sick.*

A. *Don't eat in bed.*
B. *You'll choke yourself.*

A. *Don't break a deer bone when you are eating.*
B. *You'll have a broken bone.*

A. *Don't spit out deer meat once it is in your mouth.*
B. *Next time there won't be any deer.*

A. *Don't give deer meat to dogs.*
B. *You'll have bad luck.*

A. *Don't eat the side of a sheep with a funny eyeball.*
B. *You'll go blind.*

A. *Don't eat chicken skin.*
B. *You'll get boils — bumps on your skin.*

A. *Don't eat any water animals (frogs, fish, ducks).*
B. *You'll get very sick.*

Eating in bed is frowned on

A. Don't poke holes in food.
B. You'll have ulcers— stomach trouble.

A. Don't sit on a bag of flour.
B. It will go down — you won't have anything to eat.

A. Don't eat the scum of boiled milk.
B. You'll get wrinkled.

A. Don't burn fry bread (girls).
B. You'll have a divorce.

A. Don't eat meat from a dead animal you find.
B. It will poison you — make you sick.

For a Navajo this is not so much a warning against the meat possibly being spoiled as it is a warning that you don't know what killed the animal and it might have been lightning or evil spirits or some other dangerous thing.

A. Don't waste good food.
B. Next time you'll go hungry.

A. Don't eat anything from a trash pile.
B. You'll get a bump — hunchback.

A. Don't eat raw meat.
B. It will poison you.

A. Don't eat raw potatoes.
B. You will get a lump under your chin (goiter).

A. Don't eat watermelon lying down.
B. You'll choke.

A. Don't rub your stomach after you eat.
B. You'll get a pain.

A. Don't play with your food.
B. You'll never have enough.

A. Don't let your hair touch the food.
B. You'll have hair grow in your stomach.

A. Don't eat certain parts of the sheep (boys).
B. Only ladies eat it — might get hunchbacked.

A. Don't eat when there is an eclipse.
B. You'll get sick.

A. Don't eat frogs.
B. Bad luck — bad breath.

CORN — SACRED FOOD

Corn almost certainly became important to Navajos in the fairly recent past when they moved into the Southwest where the Pueblo Indians already in residence had gotten corn from Mexico at an early time. Since it became such a staple food in the Navajo diet and allowed such sweeping changes in material culture, religion and residence, to say nothing of actual survival, it is not surprising that Navajos revered corn as a gift of the gods and invested it with great powers. In the creation story, for example, First Man and First Woman were created from perfect ears of corn. Corn pollen is used in virtually every aspect of Navajo religious life and observance. Corn plants appear in many Navajo sandpaintings and as a motif in much of Navajo art.

Before corn, most Native Americans, Navajos included, were dependent on following the herds of buffalo and other wild animals for the bulk of their nutrition. Meat was supplemented by such nuts, seeds, berries and roots as were seasonally

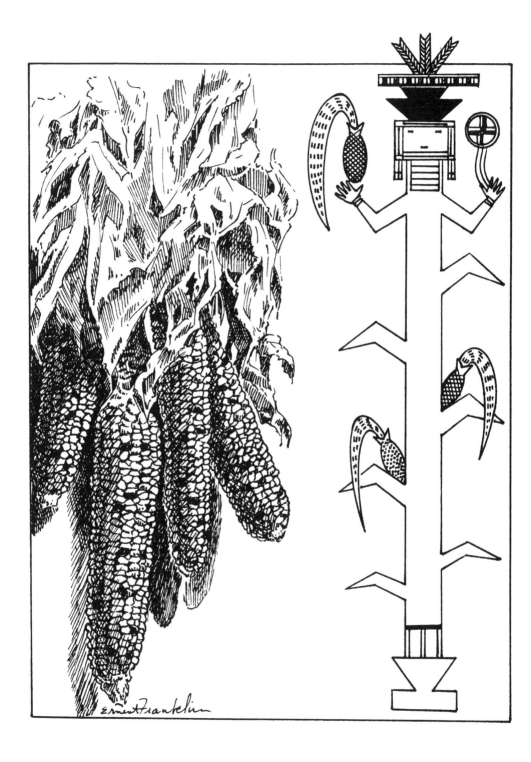

available. It was difficult, before agriculture, to build and maintain cities of any size, to have leisure enough to pursue the arts extensively, or to accumulate stores of possessions since constant movement was the norm.

Corn could be produced in surplus and stored against hard times, droughts, and cold years. It allowed such physical freedom and relative prosperity that it couldn't help but influence the arts, material culture and philosophy. It is only natural to have great respect for the plant that gave you so much freedom and security.

A. Don't drink water after you eat fresh corn.
B. You'll still be empty — the rest of the corn will freeze.

A. Don't put corn in the water.
B. It will cause a flood.

Remember the taboo against putting pinon nuts in water? The combination of food + water = cold pops up several times but the connection is not obvious except in the context of putting valuable water with other precious things — excess, in other words.

A. Don't blow on hot corn.
B. You'll lose your teeth before you are old.

A. Don't blow on corn pollen.
B. You'll get lung cancer or disease.

There are several taboos against blowing on things as well — perhaps a reference to the sacred winds.

A. Don't run around while eating corn.
B. It will choke you.

A. *Don't eat twin ears of corn.*
B. *You'll have twins.*

A. *Don't leave a pile of corn outside too long.*
B. *The sun will take it.*

A. *Don't put corn pollen in your car without the medicine man's consent.*
B. *You'll have a wreck.*

A. *Don't waste or play with corn pollen.*
B. *You'll have bad luck.*

A. *Don't put partly eaten corn back to cook when you are roasting it.*
B. *Your crop will just die out.*

A. *Don't bite on roasting corn and then put it back.*
B. *It will get cold and ruin the rest of the crop — your teeth will fall out.*

A. *Don't grind corn with a stone grinder (boys).*
B. *You might grind your penis off.*

A. *Don't shake a sack that had corn in it.*
B. *Bad luck — lose your corn — no pollen.*

IN THE CORNFIELD

A. Don't pollute the air in a cornfield.
B. The corn will puff up — get moldy.

A. Don't plant corn when you are too tired.
B. The corn will be lazy too — won't grow.

A. Don't plant corn barefooted.
B. It will be flat.

A. Don't go to the bathroom in a cornfield.
B. It will get moldy.

A. Don't plant mixed corn.
B. It won't grow.

A. Don't burn cornstalks.
B. It is the same as burning your field.

A. Don't leave corn lying around on the ground.
B. It will cry — won't be any good.

The taboo involving crying corn was recorded for the Aztecs by Fray Bernardino de Sahagun in the Sixteenth Century. Other interesting parallels may be found in the translation of his *Florentine Codex.*[15]

173

Never plant corn while barefoot

A. Don't lay on cornstalks.

B. They are sacred — produce pollen.

A. Don't plant the same seeds in the same field again twice in a row.

B. The seeds won't grow.

A. Don't drink liquor in a cornfield.

B. It will be the worst liquor you ever had.

A. Don't leave your tracks in a cornfield.

B. You'll lose your crop.

A. Don't hide anything in a cornfield.

B. The corn won't ripen right.

A. Don't eat in a cornfield.

B. You'll have an upset stomach.

A. Don't comb your hair in a cornfield.

B. Your hair will fall out.

A. Don't throw corn on the ground.

B. Your crop will fail.

A. Don't sleep in a cornfield.

B. You'll have bad dreams.

A. Don't make jokes while harvesting.

B. Your corn won't grow next time.

A. Don't throw any seeds away.

B. Your crops won't grow much.

A. Don't climb a fruit tree at night.

B. It won't have fruit — won't grow.

A. Don't point at melons with your forefinger.

B. You'll have less — they'll lose their taste.

It's not a good idea to comb your hair in the cornfield

A. *Don't eat a melon and throw the rind in the field.*
B. *They won't grow there any more.*

A. *Don't leave out squash when you plant.*
B. *You won't survive the winter.*

A. *Don't pick small pumpkins before they are ripe.*
B. *You won't grow much.*

A. *Don't make eyes for a scarecrow.*
B. *You'll go blind.*

A. *Don't use a dead person's clothes for a scarecrow.*
B. *They will come back for their clothes.*

WEAVING

The Navajos believe in the Greek maxim "Nothing to excess" believing that overdoing a thing brings bad luck as an offense to the spirits. For the same reason nothing must be too perfect. A rug or basket design with a solid border must have a break in it or flaw to let the spirit of the maker, who has spent so much time and energy, escape. It is natural that things which bring one a livelihood should also have some restrictions.

Hunting, of course, is significant for the same reasons that crops and livestock must have special care; it could mean life or death in the providing of food. Only a few taboos relating to hunting are still known, though there are quite a few which indicate the proper use of deer meat. The taboos of warfare, which even included a special vocabulary, have been largely forgotten in the hundred years since the Long Walk.

Many commercially minded weavers and other craftsmen have begun to ignore the taboos of their trades as being too restrictive. The large number of taboos relating to pottery making have been given credit for the decline of that craft, and none are listed here.[16]

A. *Don't hit anyone with weaving tools — crack the tools.*
B. *They will be paralyzed in the future.*

A. *Don't spank your children with weaving tools.*
B. *They'll get sick.*

A. *Don't have a weaving comb with six points.*
B. *Your baby might have six fingers.*

A. *Don't go between the poles of the loom when a woman is weaving.*
B. *You won't grow — cause evil — won't get much for the rug.*

A. *Don't have the loom of the weaving stand too long.*
B. *It will tire and hurt you.*

A. *Don't eat or drink while you prepare the loom for the rug.*
B. *You'll get poor — won't get much for the rug.*

A. *Don't eat while you are weaving.*
B. *It will go slow — won't be any good.*

A. *Don't weave a Yei figure with one eye smaller or one leg shorter.*
B. *It will affect you that way in later life — affect your baby.*

A. *Don't leave a Yei figure in a rug unfinished.*
B. *The Yeis will get angry — bring bad luck.*

This is interesting as a compromise taboo. *Yeis* are Holy People and as such are supposed to be represented only in the sandpaintings which are used and destroyed before sundown — but never done in any permanent form.

181

The famous hermaphroditic medicine man Hosteen Clah was one of the first to weave rug versions of the sandpaintings. In the Shiprock area *Yei* rugs and other pictorial tapestries became increasingly popular after WWII.

A. Don't be stubborn while weaving a rug.

B. It won't be worth much.

A. Don't throw weaving tools.

B. You'll never finish the weaving.

A. Don't burn weaving tools.

B. The "Yeis" will get angry — bad luck.

A. Don't weave if you don't know a weaving song.

B. It won't be any good.

A. Don't leave tools in the loom when they are not in use.

B. You won't finish right away.

A. Don't weave when it is raining.

B. It will cause the loom to fall.

A. Don't stand by the loom when it is raining.

B. Lightning will strike you.

A. Don't pass things through the loom.

B. Anything you pass through will be lost — food, yarn, beads.

A. Don't bump into or move around a loom you are preparing for a rug.

B. It will be crooked — you won't be able to get it straight.

A. Don't leave carded wool too long.

B. When you start weaving it won't like it and you'll have trouble.

A. *Don't make fun of your weaving.*
B. *It will get worse — you'll be poor.*

A. *Don't leave a loom outside.*
B. *It will collect bad things.*

A. *Don't cut off a loom once it is made.*
B. *You will have a short life.*

A. *Don't steal a rug — wool — weaving tools.*
B. *You'll never be lucky — always have bad luck.*

A. *Don't weave immoral things in a rug.*
B. *You'll be sterile.*

A. *Don't weave any taboo animal into a rug.*
B. *You will have all the bad luck associated with that animal.*

A. *Don't hang rugs out in the sun.*
B. *The sun will take it as an insult.*

A. *Don't weave at all (boys).*
B. *It will affect the reproductive organs.*

A. *Don't weave on the north side of the hogan.*
B. *The rug won't be worth anything.*

A. *Don't drag your rugs on the ground.*
B. *Causes poverty.*

A. *Don't leave an unfinished rug outside at night.*
B. *It might be witched — you won't be able to finish it or sell it.*

A. *Don't put a rug over your horse's face.*
B. *It will go blind.*

HUNTING

Obviously hunting was far more important to Navajos even a generation ago than it is today. Huge increases in population have made free hunting impossible for the same reasons it is impossible in the rest of the country, there simply aren't enough animals.

Recent jumps in the general standard of living have also made hunting less important than it was in even recent times. However, continued use of ceremonially killed and prepared buckskins in many of the ceremonies makes a certain amount of hunting necessary. Like the reluctance for Navajos to give up thousands of horses no longer needed for transportation or work animals (not to mention food), there is an emotional tie to the act of stalking deer through the forests of the high mesa country come the frosty, shorter days of fall.

Certainly there were many more taboos involved in this activity long ago, and specific taboos involved with the taking of buffalo, antelope and other large game animals. Only deer and turkey are still readily available on Navajo lands and the great care and reverence once involved with their hunting and slaying are largely things of the past.

A. Don't leave the house while your husband is hunting.
B. He won't have any luck.

Women should stay at home during hunting season

A. Don't wash your hair while your husband is hunting.
B. He won't get anything.

A. Don't sleep with your wife when you just come from hunting.
B. It will cause bad luck to your wife.

A. Don't throw deerskin or bones away.
B. They are sacred — you won't have any luck hunting.

A. Don't carry a deer you have killed without cutting its chest.
B. Bad luck.

A. Don't feed deer meat to dogs.
B. You won't get any more.

A. Don't skin a rabbit with another one looking.
B. No more rabbits — the other one will witch you.

A. Don't spit, sleep, eat in a catch pen or where one was.
B. No more game — bad luck — you'll need a ceremony.

This refers to the huge brush corrals which were once part of the harvesting of antelope on the Reservation. Antelope were wiped out in the early years of this century, but ruins of such brush fences can still be found in isolated spots. The antelope are moving closer to the reservation each year as that animal, protected now for many years, is making a comeback. I have seen antelope in the Zuni area regularly in recent years, and herds may be seen in the Flagstaff area.

A. Don't kill a deer without leaving part of it.
B. You'll never get another one.

Many Navajos say you are not supposed to bring home the

187

Ernest Franklin

The successful hunter doesn't sleep with his wife

antlers since they have a taboo against trophies or mounted heads on the walls, unlike their Pueblo neighbors. It is also against tradition to use antlers or other parts of deer (hooves, dew claws) for decoration the way other tribes do.

A. Don't throw the skin of a deer where the sheep can walk on it.

B. They will be wild like deer.

Several other places in the list there are prohibitions against mixing wild animals and domestic animals — hair, blood, skins, and the like.

CEREMONIES

In some ways almost all of the taboos are religious in nature since they are part of a right way of living. Many of them come from the myths and legends of the Navajos and thus have an indirect religious origin. The taboos listed here for the main part relate to ceremonial objects and procedures and are directed at the layman, not the medicine man who must know and observe many taboos which are not given here.

A major ceremony lasting up to eleven days and nights might involve several thousand dollars and hundreds of people. The violation of a single taboo may invalidate the entire ceremony and make it necessary to hold the entire ceremony again at a later date. The breaking of the taboo may also involve another ceremony to undo the harm that has been done.

Thus it is very important that no taboo be broken during the ceremony.

A. Don't do anything for four days after a ceremony.

B. It won't work properly — it will be ruined.

A. Don't talk while the medicine man is singing.

B. It will spoil the ceremony.

A. Don't make a noise when the medicine man is looking in the crystal — crystal gazing.

B. It will be cloudy — won't work.

A. Don't tell stories, have shoe games, play string games in the summer.

B. It will cause bad weather — you will have bad luck.

A. Don't play with a string in the summer — string games.

B. Spider woman will tie your eyes together — tie them shut.

A. Don't play the shoe game in the daytime — even in the winter.

B. It will cause a bad snow storm.

A. Don't put singing equipment facing any direction but east.

B. The sing won't work.

A. Don't sing medicine songs just for fun.

B. They will harm you.

A. Don't talk while you have a "Yei" mask on — don't spit — don't eat.

B. You will die.

A. Don't call masked dancers by name if you recognize them.

B.Evil spirits will take you away — cause them harm.

A.Don't copy a sandpainting.

B. It will give you a long illness.

A. Don't write on your body — have tattoos.

B. Only a medicine man, during a ceremony, can write or draw on the body.

A. Don't throw any religious thing away.

B. The "Yeis" will punish you.

A. Don't perform a ceremony on your own life.

B. It won't do any good.

A. Don't use salt or eat solid food when a Squaw Dance is held for you.

B. All of your teeth will fall out.

A. Don't watch the people who are putting the ashes or who are going to shoot the sample of the enemy at a Squaw Dance.

B. You'll go blind.

A. Don't tie your hair back during a blessing ceremony (girls).

B. It will fall out.

A. Don't carry the finished sandpainting any direction but east.

B. It will cause evil — won't be accepted.

A. Don't shake out a rug that carried a sandpainting.

B. It will cause a windstorm — scatter the evil.

A. Don't write in caves.

B. The holy people get angry and make you dumb.

A. Don't wear the shoes of a person who has had a ceremony.

B. You'll get what he got rid of.

A. Don't laugh about the song sung by a medicine man.

B. You'll have bad effects.

A. Don't go near or touch someone who has ceremonial paint on.

B. It will make you sick.

A. Don't pretend to be a medicine man.
B. You'll have bad luck or get sick.

A. Don't drop an arrowhead during a ceremony.
B. You'll have bad luck — get sick yourself.

A. Don't look back when you are running during your puberty ceremony (girls).
B. You will get old fast.

A. Don't pass the girl during the puberty ceremony race.
B. You'll get old before she does.

A. Don't drink milk or eat sweets during a puberty ceremony (girls).
B. Your teeth will all fall out.

A. Don't put raisins in a Navajo cake (girls).
B. You'll get blackheads.

A. Don't watch a Mountain Chant over the brush corral from outside.
B. You'll go blind.

A. Don't use any wood later that was used as part of a ceremony.
B. You'll spoil the ceremony — it won't work.

A. Don't sing songs you made up.
B. You'll get sick.

This obviously refers only to religious songs. Traditionally, Navajos had songs for almost every activity imaginable, especially boring tasks like grinding corn, weaving, smithing or horseback riding and a person was highly esteemed who could create good songs, which remained the property of the composer and could be sung by another person only with permission, though good ones would enter public domain in time.

A. Don't shake the rattle without permission.
B. It will hurt the ceremony.

A. Don't sleep during a sing.
B. You won't wake up.

A. Don't steal from a medicine man.
B. You'll lose your most valuable possession — life.

A. Don't insult a medicine man.
B. You'll suffer for it.

A. Don't look into a sweat house when it is not is use.
B. You'll go blind.

A. Don't take food into a sweat house.
B. You won't come back out.

A. Don't go in a sweat house when you are very young.
B. You'll get old too fast.

A. Don't pollute the air in a sweathouse.
B. You'll swell up.

A. Don't urinate in a sweathouse.
B. Your penis will swell up.

A. Don't enter a ceremony if you're a Christian.
B. You'll suffer for it.

WITCHCRAFT AND GHOSTS

First Man and first Woman began the practice of witchcraft according to the Navajo story, though in those days it was practiced against enemies of the people. The Navajos learned much of their witchcraft from the Spanish in the early days and several branches of the art as described by Kluckhohn show this influence.[17]

In Mexico and much of the world various forms of witchcraft are still very much alive and the descendants of the Spanish in the Southwest still know and use its power. The Hopis of Arizona also have a problem with witches as described in *Sun Chief*.[18] Those who would dismiss the darker arts too easily have not been exposed to their use. In a world filled with dangers of all sorts it is hardly illogical to assign some of them to powers we do not understand.

Modern psychology is still exploring this side of man's complicated personality. Today, more than ever, witchcraft is a major problem for the Navajos and other Southwestern Indians. Not only is a lot of negative energy generated by this antisocial behavior, but the belief in witchcraft tends to give the individual an excuse for all kinds of failures, misdeeds,

Everyone knows crossing a coyote's path is bad luck

bad luck, sloth, alcoholism and other problems. It is common to hear Navajos blame witchcraft, real or imagined, for their own problems and failures. In some cases the fear of witchcraft is so pervasive that a person doesn't even try to excel, accumulate wealth or improve things because the witches will just take everything away from you anyway.

Remember, there is no such thing in the Navajo cosmology a good ghost. If a ghost were to appear to someone in the guise of a dead relative, it would not be the spirit of the relative, but an evil power trying to get at you. For practical purposes I have not separated evil spirits or ghosts from witches here, because, by definition, a witch is a human being who emulates, imitates and otherwise behaves like an evil spirit. Witches or ghosts, they only mean misfortune to human beings. Life is very, very dangerous.

A. Don't cross the path of a coyote.
B. You will have bad luck or be in danger.

This taboo was discussed under Coyote. He is simply the messenger or omen of bad luck — as though there were a rule that the person had to at least have warning when something bad was about to happen. What they do about it is their own lookout.

A. Don't go where you hear an owl hoot at night — or look at an owl in the daylight.
B. Owls are spies for the evil spirits.

A. Don't talk to animals.
B. They might talk back to you — kill you.

A. Don't keep a cottontail for a pet.
B. They are ghosts' pet.

Never look into an empty sweat lodge

A. Don't keep a bluebird for a pet.

B. They are ghostbirds

A. Don't bother or kill moths.

B. They are spies for the evil spirits — you will jump in the fire.

A. Don't leave clothes around that have been chewed by a mouse.

B. Mice are helpers of the evil spirits — you will die.

A. Don't mention a dead person's name.

B. The ghost will come to visit you — it will bother you.

A. Don't talk about a person you don't know.

B. It might be a dead person.

A. Don't burn wood from a "chindi" hogan ("jeschaa").[19]
B. Ghosts will get you — you'll get sores.

A. Don't use driftwood for a fire.
B. It might be from a bad place — a "chindi" hogan.

A. Don't take things that belonged to a dead person.
B. The bad spirits will get after you.

A. Don't go into a graveyard or walk on a grave.
B. The evil spirits will bother you.

A. Don't touch a human bone.
B. The bad spirits will get after you.

A. Don't step on a human bone.
B. You'll get a leg ache.

A. Don't touch a dead baby.
B. It will come back to life some day.

This is as close to a reference to reincarnation as I have ever seen in Navajo lore, though I have seen claims, as mentioned elsewhere, that Navajos used to think bears were reincarnated ancestors. There does seem to be a belief, held by other southwestern tribes as well, that the spirits of babies who die at birth or in infancy do hang around the earth and wait for another chance at life.

There is a very poignant scene dealing with this topic in *Sun Chief*.

A. Don't let small children see a dead person.

B. Children are weak and it will have a bad effect on them — give them nightmares.

A. Don't wash, cut your hair, or mend your clothes for four days after a death.

B. You will kill the person all over again — you are not showing respect — the ghost will bother you.

A. Don't thank people who help with a funeral.

B. They will be the next to die — will die soon.

A. Don't stack rocks up.

B. Ghosts do that — indicates a funeral.

The traditional Navajo method of burial involved a few close members of the family of the deceased preparing the body and taking it, often by a roundabout path, to a canyon where the body could be put into a crack in the canyon wall, if possible and rocks or logs piled in front to protect the body. Where the body was placed in the ground in a grave, stones were piled on top.

A. Don't pretend to cry or pray for no reason.

B. Someone in your family will die — you are wishing for that.

A. Don't talk about killing yourself.
B. Someone else in your family will die.

A. Don't leave a broken window unmended.
B. Ghosts and other bad things will come in.

A. Don't chop wood at night.
B. Evil spirits will make you hurt yourself.

A. Don't go to bed with your hair hanging straight.
B. Ghosts do that.

A. Don't call a whirlwind names.
B. Evil spirits will get you.

A. Don't run around the hogan.
B. Only ghosts and bad spirits do that.

A. Don't put ash powder in a tree.
B. You'll see a ghost there.

A. Don't poke or dig in your ear.
B. An evil spirit might push your hand and break your ear drum.

A. Don't say "chindi" (evil spirit).
B. One will come to you.

A. Don't eat with your left hand.
B. Ghosts do that.

It is hard to tell if this is a traditional belief or one picked up due to Anglo influence. Lefties seem to get short shrift in many cultures as doing things lefthanded seems backwards or "wrong" to those who do them the other way.

A. Don't put your clothes on inside out or backwards.
B. Dead people do that — you will go crazy.

A. Don't comb your hair at night unless there is a special occasion like a Squaw Dance.

B. Evil spirits will bother you.

A. Don't wash your hair after sundown.

B. Only ghosts do that.

These are really references to the preparation of the body for burial, rather than activities of witches. On the other hand, night belongs to the bad guys and unnecessary activities are avoided in general.

A. Don't shake bedding at night.

B. It will attract ghosts.

A. Don't walk on a steep mountain alone.

B. The evil spirits might make you fall.

A. Don't eat in the dark at night.

B. Ghosts will cover your mouth or choke you.

A. Don't walk alone at night.

B. Evil spirits will bother you.

Some Navajos believe there is really no protection against the evil spirits that inhabit the darkness. The best protection is to stay indoors, preferably in a group of people.

Live a good life and take care of your personal possessions and don't carelessly leave anything — especially hair, spit, fingernail parings or blood — clothing or valuable articles where the *chindi* can molest them.

If one MUST travel in the dark, juniper ashes smeared on the face may help, or juniper berries carried in the mouth. Beads made from the husks of juniper berries found in packrat nests are strung together and may afford some protection.

Evil spirits make unloaded guns dangerous

These are often referred to as "ghost beads" for this reason.

A. Don't point an unloaded gun at anyone.
B. The evil spirits can make it fire.

A. Don't look outside at night.
B. You might see a ghost fire — bad luck.

A. Don't whistle at night.
B. Ghosts whistle at night — they will come to you.

A personal medicine song, sung softly, is considered to be all right.

A. Don't hang your clothes up at night.
B. Only "Yeis" (spirits) do that.

A. Don't chew gum at night.
B. You might bite on something bad.

A. Don't sleep with your head pointing to the north.
B. You might die — north is the evil direction — dead people lie that way.

A. Don't sleep with your head toward the head end of a sheepskin.
B. It will run off with you during the night.

As discussed, this is not so much a literal taboo as a figurative one. Putting on a skin — even of a sheep — is too much like the activity of a wolfman for the comfort of a Navajo. Suggestive behaviors are avoided on general principle.

A. Don't step on a bear track.
B. You'll turn into a skinwalker.

A. Don't try to shoot a wolf man without putting ashes on the gun or the bullet.

B. The gun won't shoot — he won't die — he'll witch you for trying to hurt him.

A. Don't let a strange dog follow close behind you.

B. You might turn into a wolf man — it might be a skinwalker.

A. Don't play with fire at night.

B. It will attract witches — you will have bad luck.

A. Don't look into a mirror at night.

B. You might see a witch or ghost — your shadow might leave you and you'll die.

Yet another mirror taboo relating to those discussed in the introduction.

A. Don't trace drawings in the sand or on rocks.

B. Evil things will use them to witch you.

Another example of the extended "track" idea. Even a person's fingerprint retains some of his identity and can be used against him.

A. Don't tell a lie about a person.

B. They might be a witch and get angry.

A. Don't tell stories about witchcraft.

B. They might come back to you.

A. Don't shake hands with a stranger.

B. He might witch you.

A rather simple explanation for the limp handshake that has disconcerted Anglos for more than a hundred years. Since

Never whistle after dark

corpse poison may be transmitted in this way, a traditional Navajo will not allow a stranger to grip his hand firmly or hug him. One of the most common, and effective, types of witchcraft involves corpse powder which may be blown into a person's face in a big crowd of people, or introduced by way of contaminated garments.

One method employed is to squeeze the poison into someone's hand — thus the fear of shaking hands with a stranger. Most Anglos are bothered by the curious limp handshake grudgingly offered by most older Navajos. It is an important mark of acceptance when a Navajo acquaintance shakes hands firmly or gives you a hug — then again, he may just be witching you. Navajos in constant contact with Anglos get over their handshake problems.

A. Don't eat anything that a stranger offers you.
B. It might poison you — witch you.

A. Don't sleep at the home of a stranger.
B. He might witch you.

General avoidance of strangers is the operative principle here. Many Navajos will only give hitchhikers a lift if they have an open pickup bed for the hitcher to ride in. These taboos shed light on a lot of behaviors which would otherwise be seen as cold, unfriendly, standoffish or a particular dislike of Anglos. White people often have a hard time getting picked up at night, for example, because their pale skin in the headlights looks suspiciously ghostly to a Navajo.

A. Don't break birds' eggs.
B. You'll get witched.

A. Don't throw hair or fingernails on the ground when you cut them.

B. A witch can use them to harm you.

A. Don't spit anywhere — especially at night.
B. The witches will use it.

A. Don't leave pictures lying around.
B. You can be witched with them.

A photo has all the magical properties of a mirror image, with the further enhancement of being more or less permanent. Like anything else closely associated with an individual, his likeness is useable by a witch.

A. Don't throw wash water out at night.
B. Witches can use it — bad luck.

It's not a good idea to step on bear tracks

NOTES

1. Cf. Steiner, *Taboo,* and Freud, *Totem and Taboo.*

2. "The Poor Turkey Girl", Cushing, *Zuni Folk Tales,* p. 54.

3. Newcomb, *Navaho Taboos and Omens,* pp. 11, 14, 16.

4. See especially Chapter XVI, "The Rattlesnake-skin Does Its Work".

5. Goodwin, p. 264. Chapters 11 and 12 are devoted to Apache war taboos.

6. I try to follow the Navajo orthography established by Young and Morgan in their various fine dictionaries of the Navajo Language.

7. Steiner, p. 20.

8. The best general discussion of the traditional Navajo world view is found in Kluckhohn and Leighton, *The Navajo,* especially Chapter 9, "The Navajo View of Life".

9. See McNeley, *Holy Wind in Navajo Philosophy.*

10. See Van Valkenburgh, *Sacred Places and Shrines of the Navajo,* and Watson, *Navajo Sacred Places.*

11. This is the underlying premise of Frances Gillmor's fine novel *Windsinger.*

12. Newcomb, *Navaho Bird Tales.*

13. Young and Morgan, *A Vocabulary of Colloquial Navaho*, p. 431.

14. See Kluckhohn and Leighton, *Children of the People* for Navajo child rearing and Bailey, *Some Sex Beliefs and Practices in a Navaho Community*, for taboos relating to pregnancy and birth.

15. Dibble and Anderson, *The Florentine Codex*.

16. See Tschopik.

17. Kluckhohn, *Navaho Witchcraft*.

18. Simmons and Talayesva, *Sun Chief*.

19. *chindi* is the Navajo word for evil spirit, *jeschaa* is the word for a hogan in which someone has died and which was abandoned or burned in the old days. It is a measure of the Navajo feeling towards death and the dead that they have a specific term for such a structure.

BIBLIOGRAPHY

Bailey, Flora L.
   1950   *Some Sex Beliefs and Practices in a
   Navaho Community*, Cambridge, Papers of the
   Peabody Museum, Vol. XL—No. 2

Cushing, Frank Hamilton
   1901   *Zuni Folk Tales*, repr. 1931 New
   York, Alfred Knopf.

Dibble, Charles E. & Arthur J. L. Anderson
   1963   *Florentine Codex*. Salt Lake City:
   University of Utah Press.

Driver, Harold E.
   1966   "Geographical-Historical versus Psy-
   cho-Functional Explanations in Kin Avoidance,"
   Current Anthropology, Vol. 7, No. 2.

Freud, Sigmund
   1918   *Totem and Taboo*. New York: Ran-
   dom House. Gillmor, Frances
   1930   *Windsinger*, New York, Minton,
   Balch and Co.

Goodwin, Grenville & Keith H. Basso, (Ed.)
   1971   *Western Apache Raiding and Warfare*. Tucson: University of Arizona Press.

Greenway, John, (Ed.)
   1969   *Folklore of the Great West*. Palo Alto:
   American West Publishing Co.

Gunnerson, Dolores A.

  1959   "Tabu and Navajo Material Culture,"
El Palacio, Vol. 66, No. 1 pp. 1-9.

Kluckhohn, Clyde

  1967   *Navajo Witchcraft*. Boston, Beacon
Press.

Kluckhohn, Clyde and Dorothea Leighton

  1948   *Children of the People*. Cambridge,
Harvard University Press.

Link, Margaret Schevill

  1956   *The Pollen Path*. Stanford: Stanford
University Press.

McNeley, James Kale

  1981   *Holy Wind in Navajo Philosophy*,
Tucson, University of Arizona Press.

Matthews, Washington

  1891   "Marriage Prohibitions on the
Father's Side Among Navajos," *Journal of American
Folklore*, Vol. 4, pp. 78-79.

  1898   "Ichthyophobia," *Journal of American Folklore*, Vol. 11 pp. 105-12. Reprinted in
Greenway, supra.

Newcomb, Franc Johnson

  1940   *Navajo Omens and Taboos*. Santa Fe:
The Rydal Press.

  1970   *Navajo Bird Tales*, Wheaton, IL, The
Theosophical Publishing House.

Steiner, Franz

  1956   *Taboo*. London, Cohen and West.

Tschopik, Harry Jr.
1938   "Taboo as a Possible Factor Involved
in the Obsolescence of Navajo Pottery and Basketry,"
American Anthropologist, Vol. 40, No. 2 pp. 257-62.

Talayesva, Don & Leo W. Simmons, (Ed.)
1942   *Sun Chief: The Autobiography of
a Hopi Indian.* New Haven: Yale University Press.

Underhill, Ruth
1953   *Here Come the Navaho!* Lawrence,
Kansas: Haskell Press, Department of the Interior.

Van Valkenburgh, Richard F. and Scotty Begay
1938-1940   *Sacred Places and Shrines of the
Navajo*, Flagstaff, Museum Notes, Museum of Northern Arizona, Vol. XI and Vol. XIII.

Watson, Editha
1964   *Navajo Sacred Places*, Window Rock,
Navajoland Publications, Navajo Tribe, Ser. 5.

Weber, Anselm
1916   "On Navajo Myths and Superstitions,"
Franciscan Missions of the Southwest, Vol. 4 pp. 38-46.

Young, Robert W. & William Morgan
1951   *A Vocabulary of Colloquial Navajo*, Phoe-
nix, United States Indian Service.
1967   *The Navajo Language.* Salt Lake City:
Desert Book Company.
1980   *The Navajo Language: A Grammar and
Colloquial Dictionary*, Albuquerque, University of New
Mexico Press.